"I have had the pleasure of knowing
wit, and passion are as clear today
ability and wisdom in this book are so welcomed. What may seem like a
window into the heart of a pastor will quickly become one into your own soul."

—Rusty George,
Lead Pastor, Real Life Church,
author of *Better Together*

"Few pastors have so eloquently written about the questions born from the
trials and tribulations of ministry as my friend Steve Hinton. *Confessions*
brings into the open what the rest of us would prefer to keep behind closed
doors. Thank goodness! Read this book and be strengthened by Steve's
counsel and encouraged by his kindness."

—Brian Jones,
Senior Pastor, Christ's Church of the Valley,
author of *Finding Favor: God's Blessing Beyond Health,
Wealth, and Happiness*

"There have been as many days in ministry that I wanted to throw in the
towel as there have been days of victorious knockouts. My friend and fellow minister Steve Hinton gets that and more. Writing with raw honesty,
Hinton has thrown down the questions we all ask from inside the helmet,
and in the journey, he has found the answers we all need."

—Tim Harlow,
Senior Pastor, Parkview Christian Church

"If the word *confession* means to speak the same, then anyone who reads this
pilgrimage will say, 'Me, too.' Former student and friend Steve Hinton walks
every preacher through the struggle between person and profession in this
self-disclosing book. Serving Christ in a fallen world is filled with ups and
downs and groans. Steve has experienced them all, and his testimony gives
the rest of us permission to experience them, too. At the end of the day, he
resolves to be governed by the bigger things that exist at the primal level."

—Dr. Mark Scott,
Preaching and New Testament/Director of Preaching Department,
Ozark Christian College

"In his excellent book *Confessions*, Steve writes with uncommon candor about the struggles so common to his calling—a calling so rarely understood by most, including many other preachers. Once you start reading this book, you will be immediately captivated both by Steve's honesty and his insights. I happily recommend this book to all who seek a better understanding of just why and how ministry is getting harder and why we need more determined leaders and preachers like Steve."

—**Dr. Alan Ahlgrim**,
Director of Fraternity Covenant Groups,
The Center for Church Leadership

"Preachers are translators. It is why we so often use a good story to communicate biblical truth into everyday speech. Jesus did it routinely. One of the most engaging qualities of Steve Hinton's story and storytelling ability is his capacity to use everyday talk to communicate grand truths. Words like *reconciliation*, *redemption*, and *justification* are on the fringe of Steve's unfolding story, but he never leverages them to make himself appear more than he really is. When he does venture into the deep waters of sanctification, Steve wraps the word in the blanket of his own story with simplicity and grace. His story is not simply the confessions of a preacher, but his story is our story."

—**Dr. JK Jones**,
Director of Spiritual Formation, Lincoln Christian Seminary,
Eastview Christian Church, Normal, Illinois

"We need answers from God beyond the entrancement of social media. Steve has given us those answers. He has written with maturity and experience beyond his years."

—**Max Goins**,
Pastor of Congregational Care, Heritage Church,
Executive Director, We-Go Mission Coalition

"Steve Hinton's honesty about ministry and himself is refreshingly raw, honest, humorous, instructional, loving, and God-glorifying. He bares his soul, brings us back to the loving arms of God, and bares his soul some more. It is obvious that he has not only been through the trenches but also understands the kingdom of God on a level that few do, but many long to.

After reading this book, you will find yourself understanding the kingdom of God more also. Though written by a pastor and especially for men, it is more than just for the man in the pulpit; it is for everyone. This will be a valuable resource in my ministry to pastors' wives as well."

—**Laura Mullenix,**
Founder, Bethnuah Ministries, author of *The Long Way Home*

"While *Confessions* does share practical tips and scriptural references, it is not a collection of research data and interviews. Rather there is an openness and authentic revealing that most of us can relate to. So if you just need encouraging, you ought to read this book by Steve Hinton. You will probably find it a most enjoyable conversation, but you will need to bring your own cup of coffee."

—**Larry Kineman,**
Christian Missionary Fellowship, Worchester, England

"Steve Hinton gives an honest look at how important and significant the relationship between a father and a son is—the scars and holes that persist for many years. Others who have grown up in a similar situation would be encouraged by his transparency and the sharing of his story and thoughts."

—**Dr. Gary Zustiak,**
Professor of Psychology and Counseling,
youth speaker

"One of my deepest convictions is that when people get real—being gut honest about all the brokenness and messiness on the inside that we'd prefer no one to know—grace begins to overflow its banks. So when a pastor or Christian leader gets real—giving us glimpses behind the clerical covering into their real humanity—well, then grace roars like a hurricane. In *Confessions*, my friend Steve Hinton (don't call him Pastor Steve) gets so real about his hurts, hang-ups, and hopes that it might make you uncomfortable. But through the pages of this book, Steve shares two profound gifts with his readers—that we are loved just for who we are and not for what we should be, and that there is joy in following Jesus, regardless of our past."

—**Michael John Cusick,**
CEO, Restoring the Soul,
author of *Surfing for God*

CONFESSIONS

FINDING HOPE THROUGH ONE PASTOR'S DOUBT

STEVE HINTON

LUCIDBOOKS

Confessions
Finding Hope through One Pastor's Doubt

Published by Lucid Books in Houston, TX
www.LucidBooksPublishing.com

ISBN-10: 1-63296-303-5
ISBN-13: 978-1-63296-303-1
eISBN-10: 1-63296-273-X
eISBN-13: 978-1-63296-273-7

Fifty percent of the royalties for this book will be donated to missions work.

Some names within this book have been changed to protect privacy.

Special Sales: Most Lucid Books titles are available in special quantity discounts. Custom imprinting or excerpting can also be done to fit special needs. Contact Lucid Books at Info@LucidBooksPublishing.com.

For my sons.
May the world be blessed with more young men like you.

TABLE OF CONTENTS

It is not the critic who counts; not the man who points out how the strong man stumbles, or where the doer of deeds could have done them better. The credit belongs to the man who is actually in the arena, whose face is marred by dust and sweat and blood; who strives valiantly; who errs, who comes short again and again, because there is no effort without error and shortcoming; but who does actually strive to do the deeds; who knows great enthusiasms, the great devotions; who spends himself in a worthy cause; who at the best knows in the end the triumph of high achievement, and who at the worst, if he fails, at least fails while daring greatly, so that his place shall never be with those cold and timid souls who neither know victory nor defeat.

—Theodore Roosevelt

Well done, good and faithful servant!

—Jesus Christ

FOREWORD

These eyes—holes of a mask.

—John Updike

I first met Steve Hinton at a church planting conference in the spring of 2004. Over lunch, I had hoped to persuade Steve and his wife, Debi, to move up to Toronto, Canada, to plant a church. I failed.

Most preachers are familiar with failure, more than they would like to admit. In seminary, aspiring pastors are told that great things await them. Ministry dreams are conceived. Professors and fellow students affirm these dreams, enthusiastically exhorting the impassioned young man or woman to become a world-changer for Christ. The enthusiastic pastoral student yearns for graduation day, craving to make an epic difference for God in their vocations as quickly as possible. But many, sometimes immediately after ordination, often much later, find themselves gripped with a sense of fatigue, inadequacy, and disillusionment that finally creeps over their lives like a smothering shadow.

Pastor and author David Hansen once observed, "The pastoral ministry is a pilgrimage through the wilderness."[1] Now, Steve reveals in his own book, with candid vulnerability, his pilgrimage—and humanity. Vulnerability can be risky, but mask-wearing is worse. Steve does us all a great service by lowering his mask. His honesty is refreshing, as is his ultimate discovery that Steve—not Pastor Steve, not Saint Steve, not pious and religious Steve, just ordinary, everyday Steve Hinton—is loved and treasured by God. I've seen God's work in Steve's life over the years of our friendship. And by no means do I see this book as the end or culmination of that work.

If you are a spiritual seeker wrestling with the idea of a personal, purposeful, and loving God, this book will help you find those next steps in understanding the difference that knowing this God—not religion—can bring to your life. In fact, this book, while part memoir, isn't really about Steve. It's about Jesus, who stated his own purpose as this: *"I have come that they may have life, and have it to the full"* (John 10:10).

If you are a "professional pastor" (Steve will be cringing at that term), this book will be like sitting down with a close friend who knows and understands the unique struggles you are enduring. Life and ministry are an apprenticeship in which Jesus, by his grace, recovers our humanity and, through our fumbling efforts, enables others to do the same.

Through the years, I have seen Steve awaken to God's bigger picture. That picture does not depend on his results or on things that we have come to wrongly equate with "successful" ministry—growing budgets, larger buildings, or swelling membership rolls. Steve has learned that God is faithful and will fulfill His purposes whether Steve's ambitions and dreams are realized or not.

Everyone who pursues a ministry vocation enters it bringing with them their own hang-ups, brokenness, and ignorance—even naivety. I have come to appreciate this quote by Dag Hammarskjöld: "You asked for burdens to carry—and howled when they were placed on your shoulders. Had you fancied another sort of burden?"[2] We should probably enter ministry with this prayer: Forgive me, Father, for I know not what I'm doing. Read on and you will see Steve confess his mess, accept God's love, follow Jesus's path, and find real satisfaction in doing so.

Finally, this book offers hope. If your ministry sails are slack, this book offers a breath of God's spirit to fill them again. As I read Steve's book, I was reminded that I cannot control the storms or even the place where my ship may come to rest. It is my job to simply raise the sails that I might catch the winds God sends. That is enough. We don't have to be heroes. The greatest act of heroism was when Jesus gave his life on the cross, walking out of the empty tomb so that his people could enjoy rest in him. For it is in Jesus alone that we can find the satisfaction of doing abundant life—in big places or small—with love for our neighbors and ourselves, and the freedom to enjoy God in the work and the love that he gives us there.

I'm glad that you have picked up this book, and I'm proud of Steve for writing it. I feel like he and I have walked a similar path. Our stories may differ in the details, but we have shared the same struggles. Masks just don't fit me well. God sees me and accepts me as I am. There is freedom in that. I pray that God uses Steve's story to give fresh hope to all who read it.

Jim Tune
President, Impact Ministry Group, Toronto, Canada

INTRODUCTION
BLOOD ON THE STAIRWAY TO HEAVEN

"Well, this sucks," I told myself. I know, preachers aren't supposed to talk that way, but maybe they should, you know, when churchy words don't seem to convey what's going on in the soul, when life just doesn't make sense. I've never been a fan of religious verbiage anyway. I especially hate it when people call me Pastor Steve. God doesn't call me that. In fact, God doesn't really look at life like that, the religious versus the secular. Sometimes, people segregate life into little controllable boxes—work, money, family—and try to schedule in God somehow. Then, they try to organize those boxes around their life, like a dentist laying out the tools before an oral exam. Each instrument is cleaned and ordered but never touch each other.

But God doesn't work that way. Every box can and should come under God's sovereign care. They all connect like threads in those huge tapestries in ancient European castles. There is a purpose to each thread, yet woven together, they unite to create a single masterpiece. To understand the intersection of God and life, we have to see that.

But where I was not long ago, everything just sucked. Maybe you've felt that way, too.

I don't remember if it was before a vacation or just normal and routine when I was at Discount Tires waiting for my number to be

1

called and looking at the guys in the garage bay. Those guys were amazing. They had it down to a system, with tunes blasting over the stereo. They were getting the job done and enjoying each other while accomplishing a purpose of which I was the beneficiary. As the minutes advanced, I almost envied them. I almost wanted their job—I mean, really truly wanted their job.

Here's the deal. I was tired of waking up every morning confronted with the pressure of others staring at me like an opposing prize fighter pushing his glove into my face. I was yearning for some relief in a big way. I just wanted to change tires all day. I'd still get up early, grab some coffee, and spend some time in the Bible and pray. But from there on, it would be totally different. I'd get to the tire shop a bit early to settle in and then change tires for the next eight hours. That's it. I'd go home and relax and hang with my wife and kids. When the weekend rolled around, I'd catch a movie, sleep in, and enjoy a church gathering, responsible for nothing. Wow! Imagine no demands, no drama, no expectations—just being there to receive.

I was tired, exhausted from dealing with the brokenness and wounds of people. Most people don't understand the life of a typical preacher. The work and emotions never end. Vacation? Yes, that's when you camp out on Saturn for a while where no one can get in touch with you. Not many pastors can afford that kind of a sabbatical. But that wasn't my real problem. Simple burnout is one thing, but I was in another country—maybe another universe. The truth is that I was tired of my own brokenness and wounds. I'd been wearing a mask for a long time, and I was just about at the end of pretending.

I knew how to play the part and was doing a pretty good job at it—smile, encourage others, and keep the sermons coming. I knew how to wear the nice-preacher hat, and it was killing me. One of the first sermon series I taught in the northwest Houston area was God's love and divine purpose for our lives. The elephant in the room, though, was that I didn't believe it for myself. There it was—all my life revolved around telling others how much God loved them but not believing it for myself. Okay, maybe he loved me, as he loves everyone. But I wasn't sure he liked me.

I was legally in the family, and I knew that was true. I knew it in my head, anyway. Yet I was in a dark place because I just didn't think God liked me. I felt as if the perfect father of the universe was holding out on me. If life were a family reunion, God was taking the kids out on an adventure while I had to stay behind and clean up the kitchen after lunch. Yes, I was in the family, but I felt like the rejected stepchild.

Where was the disconnect coming from? How much of it was true? Was I wrestling with simple envy? Yes, even preachers can be afflicted by this nasty fight for first place. I'm sure that was part of the equation. I knew guys who seemed to have the golden touch, succeeding at everything they put their hands on. Sure, we all wrestle with that in one form or another. Why is it that one person puts in the midnight oil to get the project done right, but another gets the raise because they made a better presentation to the corporate board? But there was more. What was behind my angst and mammoth melancholy? Was it just a passing phase? If not, what was the root?

I felt like a failure for not producing more. Was I? I'd been basically told that by some high-powered church management brokers. Was I just stupid? I thought that for a while. What about the dreams that I believed God had put in my heart? By dreams I don't mean simple material desires for a new car, a sure retirement, or an exotic vacation with my wife. I'm talking about ministry dreams that would help connect people to the healing power of Jesus and then help them grow. Yes, some of my dreams were truly for God's glory and the building up of others. But at this point, none of them were close to being realized.

Was it wrong what I had heard from God? If so, then maybe I was just being stupid, and we've already camped out there. Either way, I was lost at sea, drowning in the salt water, and the sharks were drawing in for the kill. Could there be any hope?

I never intended to write about my journey, but a good and wise friend, Dr. Eriko Valk, suggested I do so. Dr. V is a woman of faith, and wisdom springs from her like an oasis in an African desert. She's five-foot nothing at best, but she's a powerhouse whom I'm sure heavyweight politicians and theologians call regularly for advice. She suggested I move on this. How do you argue with wisdom incarnate?

I know many have walked much more difficult roads. I know I'm not alone in my journey, and my prayer is that something in this book might be an encouragement to another traveler along the road.

This is the story of a preacher who is just a regular guy. It's not about Pastor Steve. Just Steve. A story about someone like you. It is my hope that by walking through these pages, you'll discover that Jesus loves you, too.

CHAPTER 1
WHEN ONLY GOD SEES THE GOOD IN ADHD

There is not one square inch of the entire creation
about which Jesus Christ does not cry out,
"This is mine! This belongs to me."

—Abraham Kuyper
Netherlands Prime Minister, 1903

Adventure, with all its requisite danger and wildness,
is a deeply spiritual longing written into the soul of man.

—John Eldredge

One of my favorite places on the globe is Lake Tahoe. In early August 2004, my family and I moved to northern California to plant a church from scratch. It was then that I first discovered this hidden gem nestled amid the Sierra Nevada mountain range. After a few weeks of getting settled into our new home and signing the kids up for school, I took four days off to get away and strategize for our upcoming work. A new friend told me about a ministry that gave pastors a discount on cabin rentals in the Lake Tahoe area, so I jumped at the offer. I drove two hours to a small community just north of the lake on the California side.

My windows had been up the whole drive with the air and tunes on, so I wasn't aware of the change in the outside air quality until

I stopped to pick up the key for my cabin. Crossing the tree-lined parking lot to the office, I inhaled the fresh air, the smell of pine, lake water, earth, and nature. I had to stand still for a few minutes. That kind of euphoria had not swept over me since I was a kid camping in the mountains of New Mexico with my Boy Scout troop. It was beautiful. It was clean. It was powerful. And it reminded me of God in a very big way.

The major scientific bent today is that the earth is billions or trillions of years old. Some theologians believe in a young earth. Some philosophers believe in theistic evolution, a platform to somehow unite the theories of evolution and creationism. Honestly, I don't know exactly how old the earth is. But it sure is beautiful.

The real question of origin has to do with us. Are we merely the products of random chance, or are we something more? That leads to questions that lie at the root of our souls, if we have one. Who are we? Where did we come from, and where are we going? Is there a divine, and does he care about me? Is there any meaning to who I am, or is there no difference between me and that deer that I hit on the road a few years ago? The carnage wasn't a pretty sight.

A while back, my in-laws, who are both public school teachers, were talking about a new program in the elementary school that was running a new initiative to encourage self-esteem in the youngsters. The theme had a dolphin for a mascot, I suppose because dolphins are nice and happy. But if we're honest, if we're really nothing but evolutionary chance, then let's just face the reality that it's logically and truly just the survival of the fittest.

How do we determine purpose and value, anyway? Is the president of the United States more valuable than you or me? Well, he's got that motorcade and a contingency of Secret Service always protecting his life. As far as I can tell, there are no men in black following closely behind me with Berettas in their suit jackets to protect me. Let's face it. In the order of things regarding the United

States of America, I'm just a number. The president, on the other hand, is so much more.

This idea of preference and rank reminds me of a book I read in the fifth grade about the Battle of Iwo Jima. In the final pages was a list of all the Medal of Honor recipients for the battle. Many of the medals went posthumously to the families of the young Marines who had given their lives to save officers when an enemy grenade came in. They threw their bodies on the explosives to save the officers' lives. We are right to see the heroics, honor, and selfless sacrifice of people giving their lives for someone of higher rank.

The truth is that there was and is a chain of command, and the world values those at the top of that chain. The upper rank—the powerful, rich, and smart—are the ones with the cherished seats of value. So we often feel like the Redshirts in *Star Trek* who are always expendable extras on missions with Captain Kirk and Mr. Spock. No one wants to be the Redshirts.

If you remove the divine, it really is survival of the fittest, even if it is something you can earn or purchase. But when are you high enough? A Christian rock song asks, "If I make it, I'm a good man. Am I a bad man if I fail?"[1] I've felt like a failure a lot, and I can trace that emotional drain all the way back to early elementary school years.

For the longest time, I thought the term *attention deficit hyperactive disorder*, or *ADHD*, was reserved for parents who just didn't know how to raise their kids. Then, God gave me the poster child for ADHD in our firstborn. My son is a genius. He also has more energy than a platoon of Marines about to advance into enemy territory. Forget trying to fit him into any mold of properness and organization. Calm for him means that only two volcanoes are exploding simultaneously instead of 12. But the real awakening came when I realized that if experts were classifying ADHD when I was a kid back in the 1970s, it might have been me they were talking about. Honestly, I don't know if I had ADHD or not. My aunt and uncle tell me I was way too serious for this categorical description, and an old mentor tells me I was probably born already 55 years old. But I was clearly too adventurous for the adults around me.

I could list story after story of getting into trouble as a boy for just being a boy with too much energy and hunger for life than could fit nicely into a quiet and calm public school system. Checks for unnecessary talking in my elementary school report cards? Yup, every six weeks. Playing with fire? Do I really need to answer that one? Exploring beyond the lines, imagining inventions, and finding inventive ways of doing life were the norm for me. I kind of feel sorry for my first-grade teacher. She was actually my second-time-around first-grade teacher—I was one of those two-term first-graders. She retired a couple years after she was my teacher, and I understand why.

She probably just didn't know what to do with me, and I suffered for it. My creativity? The lesson was to cut out and paste some train cars on a piece of paper in numerical order going down the hill. But I wanted my train to go uphill. So it did. And I got an F for not following directions. The fact that I actually knew my numbers seemed irrelevant, and because I chose to be more interesting than the rest of the class, my attempt was deemed a failure.

When you're thinking of conquering the world, who has time to sit still in a reading group with a bunch of girls with pretty dresses and curls? So my teacher grabbed my chair, straightened me up, and let the class know that I needed to be restricted, just like the boy in the made-for-television movie that had aired the previous evening. The title of it was *The Boy in the Plastic Bubble*,[2] a historical drama about a boy confined to a medical tent and set apart from the rest of the world because of his immune deficiencies. I didn't have immune problems, but apparently I was deficient.

My first trip to the principal's office came after I urinated in a trashcan in the boy's restroom and another kid told on me. Let me explain for all the ladies who are holding their hands over their mouths. The mental process probably went something like this. It was after recess, and I was in a long line in the boy's room when my brain, running a thousand miles a second, noticed a receptacle not being used. Before the various parts of my brain could hold a conference call on the merits of this observation, my cerebellum pulled the trigger on the project, and I was relieving myself. So to the office I went, certifying my label as a bad boy.

When I think of my son John, me, and countless other boys, it's clear there was no evil intent in some of these actions—probably not much intent at all. Just moving at a rapid rate of speed. It's funny to hear my wife talk about this. She's a first-grade teacher and has some ADHD boy stories of her own. She didn't know what to think about our own boys, much less the boys in her classroom. I smile when I hear about them, and she knows what I'm thinking. I've told her many times that the answer for just about any hyper schoolboy is for another man to take the boys out for a wood-splitting class 30 minutes prior to doing anything studious. And Debi knows I'm right. Let's burn some energy, boys.

Many times, some boys and some girls are wired by God in such a way that they cannot fit into a regular, structured system—at least not like everyone else. But that does not mean they are defective—just different. For quite a while, I thought I was defective, and I found very little in my life to convince me otherwise.

But there are ways for overly energetic children to work out that passion and creativity. Some choose athletics. I chose a powerful Boy Scout troop that resembled more of a paramilitary organization than a cuddly group of campers. It gave me an outlet to essentially produce with my God-given energy. I excelled. As I grew into a man, I saw that my adventurous spirit was really a gift that leads me to various parts of the world and into some exciting ministry opportunities.

It took me a while to see the good in God's creation of Steve Hinton. I remember when I read *Wild at Heart* by John Eldredge for the first time almost 20 years ago. About halfway through the book, I threw it across the room because it caused a geyser of emotions to burst from within me. I felt a sense of power. Eldredge meticulously pointed out that God is much more than we can handle within our nice systems. He is too big and wild for us to manage. In God, we see both order and adventure. The cool connection is that my adventurous side is just part of his divine creation in me.

The truth is that we are all created in the image of God with different expressions of his creativeness in each of us. In Psalm 139:13, David said that God *"created our inmost being,"* and thus there is purpose to who we are. We are not accidents but rather the masterpieces of God's creative design. We also need each other in this grand drama of life to balance us out. Some people are much more organized than I am, and I value their skills and ability. We're just different. One of my good friends is an accountant, and I'm sure we annoy each other from time to time because I can't sit still and he can't catch up. But we need each other. Thus we can, and should, celebrate who we are and use our gifts to build each other up. Yes, we are all different, and those differences are needed.

The Debster, Dr. Miranda, and Our Kingdom Calling

Throughout my years in ministry, I've interacted with many doctors and medical staff and have always marveled at their giftings. Recently, I've been marveling again as we've personally walked through my wife Debi's medical journey. We've been in relationships with many highly competent medical professionals, including Dr. Erika Simpson of Houston Methodist and Dr. Leonidas Miranda, who performed Deb's gallbladder surgery. Again and again, I've noted the abilities in these brilliant people and thanked God for their skills.

Therein lies the point: God blessed them to bless others. A central theme in the kingdom of God is that we are created in the image of God. That truth defines who we are as separate from and above the wild kingdom of creation. And within that creation of humans, we find ourselves with very different gifts, passions, and abilities that are all as unique as our fingerprints. It is within those differences that we glorify God and bless others. This principle is, in fact, a key element in the old idea of a Protestant work ethic—the principle that we are created, gifted, and called to use those abilities to serve God and bless others. That brings reason and purpose to our work beyond earning a paycheck.

It also brings a proper balance to the myth of a sacred versus secular calling. In other words, some believe that a calling is an idea used for those who are pastors, preachers, or missionaries and thus engaged in a special full-time Christian ministry. Yes, there is a special calling to full-time ministry that cannot be denied. However, the problem occurs when people assume that a calling to ministry is more sacred than a calling to careers in the secular world.

This myth says that those in Christian ministry are more holy than plumbers or architects or attorneys. The truth, though, is that a calling first speaks to *who we are* in Christ and then to *what we do* in Christ. Once we see who we are as children of God, designed in his image, we can live out the passions that lie in our redeemed hearts. God works through those passions in the careers we choose to bless others and glorify him.

This uniqueness works differently in each of us. Some love working with their hands, and some love crunching numbers and logistics. Others are scientific, and some are creative. We all need each other's uniqueness, and the world is blessed all the more when we honor and praise God's creativity in those differences. So, yes, I praise God for these doctors and honor them for their efforts. I'm amazed at the detailed minds of accountants and excited by the creativity of musicians. Those differences are some of the many things that make the kingdom of God and his design for humanity so beautiful. Doctor? Mechanic? First-grade teacher, like my wife? Whoever you are and whatever you do, rejoice in it and do it with all your heart. Let's celebrate life together.

The Sacred Versus Science

But what about the scientists, physicists, astronomers, biologists, and such? I mean, if this is a book about God, isn't there a separation between rational science and faith? If you listen to the talking heads, that is certainly the idea you get today. If, on the other hand, you are also a student of history, the facts are different.

I remember reading about Johannes Kepler in high school. He was a smarter man than I am, but that's not hard to imagine, especially when it comes to math and science. I came across his name again while studying for a Christmas sermon. Indeed, Kepler was a brilliant mathematician and astronomer. You may not know this, but he was also a profound man of faith and follower of Christ. Although Kepler is credited with discovering new planetary movements and even has NASA departments named after him, he also gave serious effort to finding the star mentioned in Matthew 2:2—the star that led the wise men to Bethlehem in their search for Jesus.

Like Galileo, Newton, and other brilliant scientists of old, Kepler didn't take the path of many modern scientists who chose to reason away the divine. He didn't believe that science explains away God, but rather that science is just another tool to explore the magnitude of God through his great creation.

Kepler theorized about the planets Jupiter, Venus, and Saturn lining up at various stages and culminating in the Pisces constellation. Apparently, that only happens every 800 years or so. Kepler reasoned that this conjuncture in about 7 BC might be the star that Matthew refers to in connection with the wise men. Was Kepler right? I don't know. It could have been this constellation connection, or it could have been something else completely and exclusively divine. But it's clear from this study of Kepler that you don't have to check your brain at the door to follow Christ.

In our modern age of science and reason, it's easy to relegate God to the back seat as a household myth you can take or leave at will. But that was not the case for these early giants of the faith and pioneers of facts. To them, faith and science were not exclusive of each other. The scientific theory was a path of exploration to what God has already done.

God, Me, and Neil Armstrong

This may surprise you, but Neil Armstrong and I have a lot in common. Well, okay, maybe not a lot. But we do have some similarities. I like to tell people that I was born the year the United States put men on the moon. In fact, my birthday is March of 1969, just a few months before Armstrong's historic first step on the moon. Armstrong liked to fly, and he earned his flight certificate even before he had his driver's license. I can't claim that kind of accolade, but I still love to fly, and I try to stick my head into the cockpit to look around every time I board a plane. Neil became an Eagle Scout in 1947. I entered the ranks of the Eagle Scouts in 1985.

I think the real connection I have with Armstrong is that we are both men who believe in a God who created the universe. The news media has said very little about this, maybe because Armstrong worked hard to stay away from the cameras and the public eye. But he did acknowledge the existence of God. What many people are not aware of is that Armstrong and Buzz Aldrin took communion together before leaving the *Apollo* Lunar Excursion Module and stepping out onto the surface of the moon that historic day.

God and science are not opposed to one another. God is the author of science, and many of the great minds of the Western world believed that science was simply figuring out what God has done in creation. Armstrong was one of them.

Bigger Than Science

As I said, I don't know how old the earth is, and I'm no scientist, but it doesn't take a nuclear physicist to see some of the cracks in evolutionary platforms. I've always been drawn to the illustration of the Mt. St. Helens eruption when I was in junior high school. Within hours, days, and weeks of the eruption, huge canyons formed out of the molten rock and lava. Today, if someone dropped by, knowing nothing of the history, they could easily date those sections of earth as thousands or millions of years old according to acceptable evolutionary scales. But those canyon structures are not that old.

The big question of origin, though, is really not scientific anyway. Science may tell us how things work or don't work, but it can't define what is good or evil or of eternal value. On the other hand, if there is truth to the Genesis account of creation, then we can derive meaning from who we are and set the platform for an honest discussion about life.

It makes me think of Lake Tahoe again, or maybe the vast expanse of desert I saw through my window when I flew across Africa to Kenya for a ministry event a couple of years ago. Those places of beauty are temples of the divine and a reminder that there is purpose to the universe.

Yes, creation is beautiful, and yes, people with all their differences are beautiful. All these people and places paint an eternal canvas that illustrates the beauty and purpose of God. It's exciting to think about it. My son's hunger for an exciting life is needed in this divine drama we call life. And let's be honest, sometimes non-ADHD people are just boring. I keep telling my wife, "Sure, you could have married a more stable guy than me—an accountant or something. But if you did, your life wouldn't be nearly as exciting." She knows I'm right about that.

CHAPTER 2
AS THE ROAD TURNS SOUTH

Brokenness is the operative issue of our time—
broken souls, broken hearts, broken places.

—Samantha Power

Paint It, Black

—The Rolling Stones

We want to avoid suffering, death, sin, ashes.
But we live in a world crushed and broken and torn,
a world God Himself visited to redeem.

—Elisabeth Elliot

A week before I graduated from college, I got a call from Walter, the attorney who handled the divorce of my mother and biological father when I was in infant. Apparently, years ago, Walter and my father had agreed that if my father would stay out of my life, Walter would keep him apprised of the big headlines as I grew up. I had no knowledge of this arrangement. As Walter and I talked, I gathered that he was worried, knowing that Debi and I were about to move to Moscow, Russia, as missionaries and that I might get over there near Red Square and die without ever knowing the story of my birth father.

For some reason, I wasn't overly impressed with this opportunity. I hadn't thought much about my biological father since middle school. There were times earlier in childhood that I wondered who he was and where he might be and what he might be doing, but I suppose I just moved on. So when the call came, my reception was almost one of duty rather than delight. I felt as if I needed to connect with this man, if for no other reason than to share the love of Jesus with him as I would any other human being.

I don't know why my mother and biological father divorced. I do know that he was clinically diagnosed with schizophrenia and often went off his medication, thus making my mother's life hell. He was a visionary and a dreamer, but not quite able to function without high dosages of medication. He was broken.

Like many other boys, I grew up in brokenness. Why is it that people suffer from mental and emotional diseases and issues? Why is it that people enter into human relationships with joy and purpose and hope, only to see them crash with no plans of resurrection? Why are there diseases out there, and why do some of our friends suffer from sicknesses? Why are little girls and little boys abused and taken advantage of? I have a friend Geri who is quite the skeptic about God these days, even though she grew up in a church setting. Part of her distrust of the whole God thing is because as a young girl, her older brother's friend abused her. She'd cried to God for help and none apparently came. Something deep inside of her broke.

My brokenness was more of a progression, sort of like the gears on a bicycle left out in the rain for years. It's not one huge crash that wreaks havoc but just a constant eroding away of the good that eventually draws the bike to a standstill. At best, it ends up in an antique shop in some small town. It's there to be looked at but never used.

My mother and I lived in the mountains of Northeastern Arizona for a couple of years when I was in preschool and kindergarten. To this day, I can see the adventurous boy that I was running boldly through the big hills and small mountains behind our house. I don't remember being afraid of much of anything at that time. Exploring the new was the order of the day for me. My mom had just graduated from Arizona State University and was in her first year teaching in a small school district. She eventually connected with the band director at the high school and remarried. I now had a dad and three older sisters from his previous marriage.

I don't remember too much from this season, though some of the memories are good. He taught me how to ride a bike. For a while, we functioned as a family, but in about a year, he and my mom divorced. I drove away with my grandparents, not really knowing what was going on. The last sight of my new dad was him standing on the front porch of the log cabin home in the mountains. I was waving at him, calling, "Goodbye, Dad! See you later."

A few months later, my mother and I were situated in a small duplex in Amarillo, Texas. I was born in Amarillo, and that's why I still tell people I'm a native Texan. (There is a difference, you know, between the native born and the transplants.) My mom was teaching, and I was diving into my first-grade year of public school. I was broken and couldn't really figure things out. I was changing and becoming a little less sure of who I was.

For the next year, my mother dated a few guys, and I experienced various men come in and out of my life. One guy lived out in the country, and another let me sit in front of him while he drove his motorcycle. If I was good, he'd let me control the speed. None of these relationships lasted very long, and maybe that was a good thing. I don't remember enough about them to know if they'd have been good dads or not. But there is something that happens to a boy when he grows up without a father. He begins to doubt himself and a lot about life in general.

Sometime late that year, my mother connected with an Army vet named Jim. He was a stable guy with a consistent job. She felt I needed a dad, so the relationship continued until they finally got married. I was adopted by Jim Hinton the following year. My adopted father was a man of consistency, at least in the years I was at home, and he took care of our needs. He had a solid work ethic and protected his family.

But Jim had his own demons. He'd grown up in the house of an alcoholic father, and ultimately, as pain goes, some of his emotional dysfunctions colored my life as well. Yes, there seems to be a touch of brokenness in all of us.

Broken Assertiveness

I recall the first time I tried to get rid of my adopted father. Like any kid, there were times when I didn't want to do what I was told and didn't feel an affinity toward him. I felt that my mother, and now my year-old brother, would be better off without him. After all, I thought, I'd been without a dad before.

So the strategy in my nine- or ten-year-old brain was to create an excuse for my mom to leave my dad. My little brother and I were at my grandparents' house for the day, and the plan was simple. Because my brother was just learning how to talk, I was going to send him into the kitchen repeating a number of curse words I had just taught him. My grandmother would hear it and be appalled. Then I could blame his toddler profanity on my dad—"Oh, he heard Dad talking like that." If everything unfolded as planned, my grandmother would tell my mom, she'd respond by divorcing my dad, and I'd be free.

The plan didn't work. My brother suddenly became incapable of retaining anything I taught him. I suppose trying to use your little brother to accomplish a divorce isn't a good thing. I also wonder if maybe God had something to do with it.

There were other times that I reached out to relatives, on both sides of the family, asking if I could live with them. I just wanted to get out and figured I could find a way to make it happen.

The final battle with Jim Hinton came when I was in the fifth grade. I don't know what the tension was, but I do remember thinking that I just didn't have to put up with this anymore. "I've had it," I thought. "I've played this game with Jim Hinton long enough, and I'm sick of it." So I punched my adoptive father to let him know that he would not be calling the shots in my life anymore. My moment of rebellious independence was great and glorious—and lasted about half a second. In the time it took me to throw my volley, Dad had pinned me to the ground. I was done. He had proven once and for all that he was in charge and I would submit whether I liked it or not.

Maybe that was it, the day I realized I truly couldn't do anything. That was the day I concluded I was powerless. That was the day I knew I was broken and there was nothing I could do about it. Why did things have to go down that way? I needed to learn the lesson of respecting authority, whether I agreed with it or not. But why did this particular lesson entail the destruction of my heart?

If there is a God who is good and who made us good and unique with the positive potential to bring good into the world, then what happened? Why the evil? Why the suffering? If there is a God who created a beautiful world with beautiful people of purpose, why is there so much brokenness?

The Bible refers to these broken actions and attitudes of the heart as sin. Part of the beauty of God's creation of us is that we are endowed with a free will to choose to follow him or go our own way. The choice for self above God is sin, and sin disconnects us from God, others, and ultimately our own souls.

Part of my brokenness evolved into my doing broken things and thinking broken thoughts. As I grew, I started hurting and breaking others as well. Yes, there was and is evil in the world, and I was contributing to it.

The Dark Ages

I never went to any of my high school reunions, partly because most of my real friends came after high school. I went to a junior college for a year after graduation and then to Ozark Christian College in another state. There, I began making friends who were in my field and had my same passions. Those people from high school seem so far removed from my life today. There are a few guys I had strong friendships with back then, and we do touch base from time to time, but that's about it. It's just life. I suppose the real reason I avoid high school reunions is that I was an insecure and unfocused guy who hurt some people back then. I was a jerk at times, and I did some people wrong.

In college, I put off taking psychology until the last moment and ended up in a class with a bunch of freshmen and sophomores. I was already married with a part-time ministry, and most of those students were still living in dorms with all the action and drama that go along with early college life. Toward the end of the semester, we had to turn in a paper in which we basically psychoanalyzed our life story. I referred to my high school years with this subheading: The Dark Ages.

Sure, there were some fun times. I enjoyed marching band, and I actually got two or three A's in classes such as history, government, and sociology. Math and science? Not so much. Like many teenagers, I was mostly living to ease the pain. I never got drunk or did drugs, but I went through a number of bouts with depression. Listening to a constant repertoire of Pink Floyd didn't help much. I also became sexually active, something I still regret. I could list all the reasons I went down that road—how the root issue of my sexual longings was really a cry for emotional and spiritual help. That wouldn't be a far stretch, considering many theologians have made that connection. In his 1945 novel, *The World, The Flesh, and*

Father Smith, Bruce Marshall noted that "the young man who rings the bell at the brothel is unconsciously looking for God."[1] Yes, there is a clear connection to this. However, no matter what my hurt was, the truth is that I hurt the girls I was with. I make no excuse. I may have been broken, but I also added to the brokenness of the world.

Indeed, there is brokenness all over the place because of people's poor decisions, for decisions can leave lasting results for generations. The story is even more distressing in that no matter how much money and government we throw at many of these issues, the root of evil still remains. It continues on because the real issue is in the heart.

The latest illustration of this is the huge media craze over a bunch of overpriced NFL players taking a knee during the national anthem before their football games. The knee-taking and fist-shaking of these athletes are directed at racial issues in the country. While their actions make for a great social and political stunt, they are missing the mark on what will really bring serious change.

Are there racists in America today? Is racism an evil thing? Sure. But let's look deeper. Consider that, at least to my knowledge, there are no remaining laws in 2018 that prevent anyone of any race from doing anything that any other American citizen can do. America, through the dream and work of great people like Martin Luther King, Jr. and others, has corrected the legal system to prevent racial discrimination in the workplace. However, racism as an attitude still exists. The problem is so much deeper than forcing someone to do or not do something. The problem is in the heart. It has always been in the heart.

Throughout history, mankind has hated mankind. The English persecuted the Irish. Ethnic Russians looked down on Crimean Tatars. Various ethnic groups in Africa have attempted to wipe others out, and some of the Native American tribes such as the Comanche were incredibly violent toward other tribes. The hatred in the human heart is not something on which the history of America has a corner on the market. Humans still hate humans.

We try to do better, and that is good. Unfortunately, even on our best days, if we're honest, we just can't be good enough. Even trying to define what is really good is a chore as we debate the issues of goodness all the time.

The hard part, though, is that we can't even maintain our own goodness. We try to set a standard, but then come the days when we don't keep our own rules. We're nice in traffic one minute, and the next we're cursing the jerk who cuts us off. Then, there are days when our schedule falls apart, and we end up being the jerk trying to regain control of our day.

No, while God did make things good, we know how to screw things up. Despite the evil in the land, somehow God continues to make his presence known in many hidden ways.

Threads of Grace amid the Garbage

I was in a large Boy Scout troop from about the sixth grade through early high school. The difference between Troop 80 and other Scout troops was probably the large number of men committed to the cause. Because of their dedication, our troop rose to one of the largest in our area, if not the whole state of Texas. Through hard work, patience, persistence, and strategy, the troop incorporated and even built its own meeting hall. Very few Boy Scout troops achieve such stature. The other troops in the area hated us. Of course, that just made us more proud of who we were. One of my friends, who was an Eagle Scout with another troop, always talked like we were the Imperial Guard from *Star Wars* or something. We were big and tough and victorious at field day events. Indeed, it takes a strong commitment from a solid group of men to create something like that.

I believe that Troop 80 was one of those treads of grace that God brought into my life. I didn't learn much from my dad, but I learned a lot from the men in this troop. While I hunted for meaning from my adopted dad, mostly coming up empty-handed, there were so many times when God seemed to bring these men along to encourage me.

Despite everything, there were little hints of hope from events and people who dropped in on my life from time to time in ways that made me think that quite possibly there was a God out there someplace. Toward the end of the book of Genesis, Joseph says that while his brothers meant evil for him, God secretly used their choices to bring him into a place of authority to save his family and the world.

Another staggering story comes from Corrie ten Boom, who survived the Nazi Ravensbrück concentration camp in World War II. Corrie and her sister Betsie were sent there from Amsterdam after being captured for hiding Jews in their home. She shares her story in her book, *The Hiding Place*. At one point, Betsie expresses gratefulness for the fleas in the bunks because the fleas kept the camp guards from coming into their rooms to rape them.

Even though I do not consider my adopted dad to be a major mentor in my life and I do connect some brokenness to how he treated me at times, I still learned some principles from him on sacrifice and how to protect my family. To this day, I always make sure my wife's car is taken care of because that's what Dad did for my mom. He had a good work ethic, taking on two jobs at once for a while, and I learned from that.

Yes, there was and is brokenness. But there were always tiny rays of light that pierced through the darkness, like those moments in the mountains when the sun shines through the clouds during a late afternoon shower. Yes, it seemed like there just might be a God after all, and a good one at that.

CHAPTER 3
THE MAGIC IS REAL

I know men, and I tell you that Jesus Christ is not a man.
Superficial minds see a resemblance between Christ and the founders of
empires, and the gods of other religions. That resemblance does not exist.
There is between Christianity and whatever other religions
the distance of infinity.

—Napoleon Bonaparte

The Word was made flesh and dwelt among us.

—Apostle John

How much happier you would be . . . if the hammer of a higher God
could smash your small cosmos.
The Christian ideal has not been tried and found wanting.
It has been found difficult; and left untried.

—G. K. Chesterton

Early on in our church plant in Northern California, I canvassed neighborhoods to spread the word about what we were doing. Rather than knock on doors, I usually stuck a card in the door or left a door hanger to get the information out. I didn't want to get in anyone's face without their interest. When I'm hanging with my family and someone rings my doorbell to sell something, I don't want them getting in my face. I'm nice and all, but I simply tell them we're not interested.

There were times, though, when I did talk to people. If someone was standing in the doorway or front yard, it was kind of obvious that I was there. I like talking to people—most of the time—and I'm really good at it, especially when I'm in the zone. Usually, I'd start my conversation with a big smile and something to the tune of, "Don't worry, I'm not selling anything." That usually sets everyone at ease. I'd just introduce myself, hand them a card, and let them know we were in the area if we could do anything for them. Sometimes, that led to further conversation, and sometimes, I just got a polite thank you with their eyes really saying, "Okay, I was nice, now please leave." What I know is that even if there was no immediate conversation, there were times in the future that I'd run into those folks—when they were in a tough bind and looking for a church or some kind of religious expert—and they'd remember the nice guy who gave them a card.

I tried to hit all kinds of neighborhoods and cultures. The cool thing about places like Sacramento and Houston is that you have multiple cultures, people from different ethnic backgrounds, living close to each other. I love that. One afternoon, I was heading up the row of a small trailer park doing my deal when I stopped at one of the last units on the trail. It was a pleasant day, and the occupant, a guy in his late 30s to early 40s, had his door wide open, reading while a cool breeze drifted into his home. The opportunity was right there to meet someone new and see what might evolve.

With perfect rhythm, I stepped up on the porch, said hello, and assured the guy that I wasn't selling anything. With an inquisitive but not annoyed look, he put down his book and walked over to me. I told him I was with a new church in the area and that we were here to help. You know, the regular stuff. As quickly as my words hit his head, his attitude changed. He said I was brainwashed like every other religious person in the world. Nothing violent or anything, but he quickly threw up his arms and returned to his book and chair as though I no longer existed. I made some pleasant responses and left knowing full well that this was not a guy open to debate or inquiry.

I don't know this guy's story, but I can understand how people's backgrounds, wounds, or life stories might lead them to believe that someone like me is nuts. I mean, there are indeed a lot of really strange, scary, and irrational beliefs out there. Back in 1997, a group called Heaven's Gate committed mass suicide, believing that their souls would be picked up by an alien spaceship that was following in the trail of the Hale-Bopp comet that was crossing the atmosphere that year. Later, in 2008, Bill Maher, a comedian and social and political commentator, starred in the movie *Religious*, in which he worked to disprove Christianity and other major world religions. In one conversation, he likened a god who could hear all of our prayers to believing in Santa Claus, which we all know is ridiculous. The idea of this rotund guy in a red suit visiting all the homes around the globe in one night to deliver presents to good girls and boys just falls into the fun idea of children's magic and fanciful stories.

I kind of like magic in a way, at least adventures with magic in them. In late elementary school and junior high, I played *Dungeons and Dragons*. The best games were the ones with adults who let me join in. There were some Friday afternoons at Sam Houston Jr. High School that were pretty much a blur because my head was preparing for the adventurous gathering that evening. I never had a wizard for a character, but I certainly wanted to have one on my team. There were times when I was pretty sure of a pending orc attack and having a wizard handy was just common sense. The adventure of it made me feel like life had so much more to offer.

I recently watched the second half of *The Return of the King* with my kids. I love that third movie in the *Lord of the Rings* trilogy and really anything from J. R. R. Tolkien and C. S. Lewis. Many people who love Tolkien and Lewis literature don't realize that both men were not only incredibly brilliant but also serious believers in Jesus Christ and the Bible. Both of them, much more so with Lewis, wrote biblical themes into their stories right under our noses.

In the cinematic adaptation of Lewis's masterpiece, *The Lion, The Witch, and The Wardrobe,* Aslan, representing Jesus, goes to the Stone Table in Edmond's place. It floored me because I knew the deeper meaning. So it is with the rest of Lewis's writings and Tolkien's *The Lord of the Rings.* Yes, it's all fiction, but it conveys something deep, something that each of us secretly cries out for way down in the catacombs of our innermost beings.

They're the kind of stories that, as Rich Mullins used to sing, "make a man walk straight."[1] When we read, hear, or watch stories of magic, bravery, nobility, and adventure where the underdogs outshine evil, we are touched deeply in a way we can't quite understand. Something of another realm grabs us. Lewis and Tolkien were neither the first nor the last to employ that kind of story imagery.

The greatest user of metaphors was Jesus himself. But Jesus was not writing for money or even to tell a great story, but rather to convey a very deep reality. The thing about authentic Christian spirituality is that it is so much more than escaping the penalty of our sin through the redeeming mission of Christ. It's about entering a newer and bigger reality.

Naysayers argue, "Come on, Steve, get your feet in the real world." But I contend that if the message of Christ is true, then we can't get our feet into the real world. Jesus spoke of the kingdom of God and the kingdom of heaven as something that existed then, now, and for all eternity. He described something that's greater than America, the United Nations, and the lines we draw on maps. He described something that's active in the hearts of all who would follow him and thrive throughout all eternity.

I think that deep down, all humankind is yearning for something like that. Why else is NASA spending a gazillion dollars trying to find life in outer space? Why is there that kind of searching of the cosmos and the soul? I believe it's because we long for something bigger than ourselves. Jesus spoke about the kingdom. He spoke about the reality of ragamuffin women and men of faith following hard after him with his rule in their hearts. That's the kingdom. That's what real Christianity is all about. It's not a bunch of proper rules to be kept; it's a life of adventure to be lived.

Phone Call to God

One of my first real memories of thinking about God came when I was in preschool in Arizona. I didn't know much about God, but I had a sense of the divine, something or someone so much bigger than I. Although I don't remember a lot of God conversations, I know we had a regular practice of praying something routine before I went to bed each evening. We also attended some form of a regular church service. Beyond that, I don't remember much until that one afternoon when I decided to make something happen.

I wanted some answers, so I decided to talk to God, or at least try to. I had some questions for him. Not too serious. Just the type of things a five-year-old comes up with, which are truly pretty serious. I wasn't sure how to make the communication happen until I remembered that there was something special about dialing zero on the old rotary telephone. When Mom was in the other room, I picked up the receiver, gave a quick dial to talk to God, and waited for the appropriate angel to pick up and patch me through. Then, just before the operator got on to laugh or rebuke this little kid, I got scared and hung up. I mean, having a phone conversation with God is a big deal.

I was not only afraid but possibly a bit ashamed to attempt to talk to someone as big as God. If we go back to the creation account in the Bible, one interesting piece of history is that before sin entered the picture, Adam and Eve were both naked and without shame. The feeling of insecurity came after they sinned. Yes, they were broken. There is brokenness around the globe, in the pages of history, and in our own hearts. And because of that, all are drawn to things that seem magical because we long for healing. We long for God deep within our souls even though we might not be brave enough to admit it.

As I remember, the first time I tried to reach out to God was when I first truly connected to God. It was on an Easter Sunday afternoon when my uncle called me back to my room to talk with me. I'm not sure, but I may have thought I was in trouble at first or something. You see, my uncle, the one married to my mom's sister, is probably the biggest role model in my life. Above all men, I respected him the most, and getting called out by a man like that is no small thing.

What happened, though, was the divine connection point that changed my life. Eric, my uncle, who is an attorney, systematically walked me through some scriptures that demonstrated my helpless condition before God. He explained that God reached down from heaven to give me Jesus and rescue me from my condition. He gave me the rundown on what authentic Christianity is all about. That thing that people call born-again Christianity now made sense. It was clear. I saw what Jesus did for me on the cross, that he died for my sin. I reached out to Jesus and was baptized the following Sunday at a big Baptist church in my hometown.

That phrase, born again, comes from John 3, a passage in which a religious expert is trying to figure God out by living a legalistic lifestyle. Jesus stops him in his tracks and tells him that what he needs is a new spiritual birth, to be born anew, or again. I knew I was changed deep within, and I knew there was something different about life. Despite all the damage and shame from brokenness, I saw that Jesus came to make things new.

Jesus paid the penalty for my sin on the cross, and I got that. He rose again, and history is replete with evidence of that resurrection, evidences that Bill Maher and similar skeptics refuse to examine. I suppose, although Bill and I have never talked about it, that the main reason people choose not to honestly look at the claims of Christ is that to do so would force them to admit their need, that they have sinned against a holy God. But when we get to that place of honesty, God moves in and changes our hearts in ways that magic never could. Yes, still to this day and sometimes in sermons, I refer back to the time when my uncle called me out and when my life—no, my eternity—changed.

Does It Work?

I have a confession to make. For a long time, I've shied away from the term *fundamentalist*. I've said, in no uncertain terms, that I'm *not* a fundamentalist. Now, I'm not so sure. The issue with the term is that the only time we see it in print or conversation these days is when it is used to describe sects like the Westboro Baptist Church cult or an Islamic group that wants to take over the world. You see my dilemma?

The problem is that the term is placed on anyone who opposes gay marriage or any social pillar that the politically correct left holds sacred. In essence, the media have beaten the dead horse of the Westboro comparison to such an extent that the true ideals of fundamentalist thought are now unrecognizable.

While some of the original fundamentalists did refuse to fellowship with those they did not agree with, they never endorsed nut jobs that held "God hates fags" signs at protests. The true essence of fundamentalist thought is light-years away from self-righteous legalism.

The original seed of fundamentalism arose in the late nineteenth century with the intent to maintain the fundamental doctrines of

Christianity, such as the authority of scripture and the divinity of Christ. The movement was in response to a number of liberal theologies creeping into the church, theologies that denied those foundational beliefs. The first formal declaration of fundamental teaching was in 1910 at the General Assembly of the Presbyterian Church, in which only five major truths were put forward. Other areas of disputable practice were ignored, and these five were considered the fundamental doctrines of pristine and ancient Christianity.

1. Biblical inspiration and the inerrancy of scripture
2. The virgin birth of Jesus
3. Christ's death was the atonement for our sin
4. The bodily resurrection of Jesus
5. The historical reality of the miracles of Jesus

I'm not a labels guy. I'm just Steve. Not Pastor Steve. But if pinned to the wall, I don't think I'd shrug away anymore from the term *fundamentalist*. I believe those basic truths and all the good that flows out of them. Yes, true fundamentalism does oppose gay marriage. In addition, though, if fundamentalism is really all about holding fast to the core of authentic Christianity, then there are also some beliefs and practices that, when lived out, actually bring a blessing to those around us. For that reason, it just might not be a bad idea to recover the term from those who have hijacked it for their own social and political purposes. Below are 10 other traits that describe people who cling to the essential fundamentals of Christianity and what they practically bring to the world.

1. Fundamentalists have a love for everyone. They love God and love others. Even in controversy, they speak the truth in love. They will love with actions and not merely words.
2. Fundamentalists hold to the foundational doctrine of creation and the creation of man in the image of God. Because of this, they see value in all humankind. True fundamentalists

will care for fellow humans no matter where they come from or what their ethnic, racial, or economic backgrounds are. This multi-colored canvas is essentially a picture of God's design for the global church. In addition, because of these foundational doctrines, fundamentalists are passionate about sharing the love of Christ with as many people as possible in as many ways as possible.

3. Fundamentalists honor God's design for marriage as being the union of one male and one female for life. For that reason, fundamentalists work for the tireless commitment to the marriage union and oppose no-fault divorce that has become so prevalent in our day.

4. Fundamentalists work to strengthen the family as God's best design in which children can be nurtured and brought up by a father and a mother.

5. Fundamentalists have compassion and care for widows, orphans, and even infants in the womb. They likewise care for unwed mothers facing an unexpected pregnancy.

6. Fundamentalists also have concern for the poor and suffering around them. They function like the first Christians who brought aid, even at the risk of their own lives, to the sick and dying rather than running away from them. We see this time and again during national emergencies and tragedies. Just take a look at who is first on the ground and stays the longest to help with hurricane recovery and the like. It's the church—the real church—those who are changed from the inside out and believe the fundamental call of Jesus to love God and others, those who are not looking for cameras and spotlights. They're out there in the mud helping others as Jesus helped them.

7. Fundamentalists commit to praying for and submitting to the government. The only exception and allowance for civil disobedience is if the state demands the denial of Christ.

8. Fundamentalists love their church and support the universal body of Christ. In our present consumer culture in which people look for what the church can offer them, true fundamentalists commit to serving others with their God-given abilities instead of looking to be served.

9. Fundamentalists believe the Bible is the inerrant and inspired word of God. Authentic fundamentalists read their own Bibles on a regular basis instead of relying on the spiritual work of others. They submit to the teachings of Christ rather than forcing the Bible to submit to their own personal experiences.

10. Fundamentalists confess their own need for Christ. Are there problems in the world? Yes! However, a person who truly follows the fundamental teachings of Christ will freely admit that problems begin with themselves first and foremost. They are no better than anyone else. They have blown it and depend 100 percent on the grace of Christ, boasting of absolutely no merit of their own.

Fundamentalist? While ground-stomping for this title is not my first priority, at the end of the day, I no longer feel the urge to dodge the term but rather hope we can recover what it really means and champion the fundamental truths of Christ that ultimately are the only real hope for humanity. The focus in authentic fundamentalism is not attacking the opposition but rather offering up the truth of Christ in both communication and practical love. That is the true hallmark of those through the ages who have held to the fundamental teachings of Christ. Looking again into the past, the original orphanages and hospitals were created by people hundreds of years ago who would be considered fundamentalists by today's dialogues. To be in the same pool with those great women and men of the faith is not a bad thing.

The Calling Is Not Returned Void

Not only does the magic work practically, but it also works super-naturally. The true Christian journey is not something merely hoped for in the future. It's experienced by trusting and following God's lead today.

Shortly after I gave my life to Christ, I sensed that he was calling me to full-time Christian ministry. I can still remember being with my aunt and uncle in a really big church service, listening as best as I could to the preacher and sensing God telling me that I would be preaching someday. I wondered, especially after some of the dumb moves I made in high school, "Could God, would God, use a failure like me?"

I debated the answer to that question a lot during my first semester at Bible college. A big uncertainty laid on my heart, and I probably drove some of the more stable students nuts with my constant worrying about my calling. Yet God was faithful and answered my prayers. Just a couple of weeks before Christmas, I got the answer I needed. It was about 6:00 p.m., after I had cleaned up from my part-time job. None of the other guys were on my dorm floor. I walked into my room alone to change and head to the cafeteria for dinner. Then, like no previous time in my life, I stopped in the middle of my room and felt as though God were saying, "Steve, you are exactly where you need to be."

It wasn't an audible voice or anything like that. It was simply an overwhelming peace that, indeed, God was directing my path. I needed that assurance to push forward beyond the doubt. The funny thing is that over the past few years, when I've felt like throwing in the towel on this ministry thing, I've looked back at that occasion and reminded myself that God is still in charge, even when I can't see it.

Despite everything going on, God was still in the mix of my life. The voice that spoke to me when I was 12 or so about preaching someday still had a plan. I didn't know what it looked like, but at least I kept going.

Keeping going wasn't just about staying in Bible college. It was also about preaching. Did God really call me to that? Sometime early in my second semester at Bible college, I lifted up a prayer of faith with this little request: "God, if you really want me to preach, then give me an opportunity."

I was in the school cafeteria waiting my turn in line the following day when the secretary for the head of the missions department came by, got my attention, and asked if I'd be interested in going with some other students to another church to lead all the morning services. The kids' classes were taken care of along with the worship service; they just needed someone to preach.

Well, let me think about it. No, I didn't have to think about anything. It was clear. I couldn't believe the answered prayer and that early testimony of God's providence, demonstrating that despite humanity or even myself, he still has a way of moving and directing the steps of those who pursue him. The truth of the matter is that we all have a calling in our lives, and even when we blow it, God is still waiting to pick us up and put us back on track when we're willing to follow and do life his way.

A Wife to Call My Own

I always assumed I'd be married someday—except on at least two occasions. The first was in the first grade—my first year in first grade, that is. Somehow, I was leading a group of boys in an army whose sole purpose was to capture the girls and throw them in a dungeon. Who needed girls, anyway? That phase didn't last too long. The second was the summer between my year at junior college and my freshman year at Bible college. I had just come out of a marriage engagement, and I was in one of those seasons of life when it seemed like God, in some kind of loving way, had hit me upside the head with a spiritual two-by-four to get my attention. I wondered if I would ever get married and seriously contemplated the idea of purposefully remaining single and celibate for the rest of my life as I served in some tough mission outpost of a super-underdeveloped country.

That was the thinking I had when I left my hometown for Joplin, Missouri, to follow a call to Bible college and full-time Christian service. That is what I expected. But again, God moved his magic, and in his providence, I found myself in a class with a young woman who would become my wife two years later.

It was actually quite a while before I asked Deb out. At first, I thought I'd never have a shot at her. But I took the chance, asked her out, and she said yes. She also said yes at the altar in June 1991. This past summer, the Debster—as I call her—and I celebrated our 27th anniversary. With all that time connected to the wife of my youth, I'm a much better man today.

In thinking of all this and more, I'm reminded of John 10:10 where Jesus said, *"The thief comes only to steal and kill and destroy; I have come that they may have life, and have it to the full."* That's what I experienced. Yes, this whole God deal is real—the hope, the healing, the purpose, and pleasure of knowing God. I know that, and it's true. Maybe that's why I wanted to be a preacher in the first place.

CHAPTER 4
HUNTING FOR DAD

*It is my hope that my son, when I am gone, will remember me
not from the battle but in the home repeating with him
our simple daily prayer, Our Father Who Art in Heaven.*

—General Douglas MacArthur

*The search after the great men is the dream of youth,
and the most serious occupation of manhood.*

—Ralph Waldo Emerson

Be watchful, stand firm in the faith, act like men, be strong.

—Apostle Paul

It's been said that our concept of God is connected with the relationship—or lack thereof—that we have with our fathers. There is some truth to that statement. I don't always know what to do with Father's Day. For some people, that day means a powerful time of positive reflection because their dad is great. Others, though, approach Father's Day with a yawn at best. Either way, I typically look at this confused occasion as an opportunity to teach about God's design for fatherhood and the family. Dads are influential and important beyond measure. When I talk with solid leaders, I like to ask them about their fathers and their relationships with them. If I'm studying the life of a great leader from the past or one presently alive that I just can't get close to, I still try to uncover something in connection with their fathers. Almost without exception, the great kingdom leaders that I know had a good relationship with their dads. He was a tremendous part of their inner formation.

My story is not too shiny in that department. When people ask me about my father, I sometimes jokingly reply, "Well, which one?" I suppose I could categorize my journey with dads in the following ways:

1. Legal Dad. He would be Jim Hinton, who married my mom when I was about seven and then adopted me a year later. Dad paid the bills and had a good work ethic. But the only advice I can ever remember getting from him was this: "Steve, I don't care what you do when you grow up as long as it's legal." Thanks, Dad, I'll try not to disappoint you on that one.

2. Bio Dad. Cary Collins would be this guy, and he and my mother were divorced before I was a year old. I didn't meet Mr. Collins until right before Deb and I moved to Russia in 1994.

3. Intermission Dad. This would be the guy my mother was married to for less than a year when I was in kindergarten. The problem here was that his three daughters targeted mom as the evil stepmother, so they all parted company. I think I actually liked this guy. He's the one who taught me how to ride a bike.

4. Commercial Dad. Commercial Dad is the collective group of men Mom dated before Legal Dad. These guys were in my world for a short time, tempting me with the idea of

fatherhood. I particularly liked the one with the motorcycle, or maybe it was just that he let me ride in front of him on the bike and control the speed.

5. Wish Dad. This dad comprises all the men I knew who made me wonder, "Wow! That would be cool if he were my dad." But they were not. They had sons of their own.

So when it comes to Father's Day, I don't think a whole lot about those who wore the name in my life. I do, however, think of the men that God brought into my journey to mentor me at various stages, and I'm thankful for them. I think of God's design for the family and challenge myself to be the dad to my kids that I never had. But I also stop and remember the words of Jesus early in his ministry regarding a father.

The disciples asked Jesus point-blank for advice on prayer. Without missing a beat, Jesus opened up with what we know as the Lord's Prayer and modeled addressing God as *"Our Father in Heaven"* (Matt. 6:9). Father in heaven? That's not too far out for some. Their relationships with their earthly fathers were great, and the expansion to a heavenly father, an eternal father, makes sense. But for many, that's just a little too far of a stretch to be comforting. Donald Miller, the author of *Blue Like Jazz*, once said that if God is our father, then maybe he made a marketing mistake. Don said that because his earthly father had deserted him as a boy and he had not yet received healing from the pain.

The idea of a father in heaven is something I get intellectually. The original word choice that Jesus made conveys the idea of a large and loving father who compassionately reaches down to care for his child. My head gets it, but my heart doesn't always follow, and I can feel the pain of many who have voiced questions—questions like "How can I trust this idea of a heavenly father when my earthly dad, or maybe no dad, was so untrustworthy?" Even if we begin to make the theological connection, there still seems to be a cry in our hearts for resolve on at least three tensions:

1. Does God like me? Sure, God loves me, but come on, God loves everyone. The question is this: Does he like me beyond the numbers of humanity?
2. Is God proud of me?
3. Can I trust him with my future, my calling, my ministry, and my life? The list goes on.

Yes is the answer to these questions. Sometimes, it just takes a step of faith and time for all the pieces to fall into place. The reality, though, is that the God of all creation really has made a way through Jesus for us to be his adopted daughters and sons. When a person is born again into the kingdom of heaven, the God of heaven becomes that person's eternal father. So a father in heaven is not like an earthly father, even on his best day. He is above them. He is perfect and powerful and without dysfunction.

This father in heaven really does feel all those affirming things toward us and will, indeed, reach down and heal all who will come to him. I don't always get it right in my emotions, but in faith, I'm daily pressing forward. I'm making the choice to call the God of all creation my father and continually reach out to him. After all, Jesus said I could.

A Dad Like That

News stories about Russell Wilson flowed almost immediately after the Seattle Seahawks won the Super Bowl on February 2, 2014. Like many Christ-followers, I was impressed with his attitude and desire to give God the glory, believing in the talent God gave him. Wilson was right on, as even our breath is a gift from God. But another point that struck me was what Wilson said about his father. He referenced his dad a couple of times and specifically noted how his father would purposefully look at challenging situations and ask, "Why not you?"

When I heard that, it all came together. That kind of fatherly encouragement is something I've observed, not only in Wilson's life but in the lives of many other great leaders. They had dads who believed in them.

Confidence is a foundational building block in leadership development, one that is sorely needed in our culture. When a father or other positive male role model speaks to a young person about a positive future, his words are of incalculable worth. You can't measure how important confidence like that is to a boy or young man. Many people in our day grew up without that blessing, and I can relate to that. But all of us can be encouraged to know that there is a *"father to the fatherless"* (Ps. 68:5), one who calls us out of fear and into courage. No matter what our background is, we can know God and his encouragement in our lives and see a future greater than we've ever imagined.

As leaders today, we can look at those coming behind us and speak positivity into their lives. What we saw passed down from father to son in Russell Wilson's life is a rarity today, but it doesn't have to be that way. For my kids, I look for opportunities to speak even small positive words, not only to them but also to kids on my block and around me. Just one man speaking a positive message of potential victory into the hearts of others is just what they need, and it might even be enough to change the world.

The need for confidence is so crucial for men. Obviously, women need that instilled in them as well, but maybe my wife can write a book on that one. This is for the guys who live in a culture that doesn't always encourage them to be guys, at least not the guys that God created them to be.

Alternative Manhood

A few years ago, my friend RT and I were running a live webcast on Sunday nights. We started *Sunday Night Discussions* out of a desire to recognize and address some real and tough questions people, especially young people, have about God. We covered issues such as evidences for God, the Bible, purpose, and manhood.

Shortly after the 2014 Winter Olympics, we hosted the two co-founders of an amazing ministry called Marked Men for Christ. The title for our show that night was "Alternative Manhood," which I kind of stole from a sports commentator.

According to Skyler Wilder, who writes for NBC, alternative manhood looks like David Wise who tore up the half-pipe free-style ski event for a gold medal in the Olympics. In Wilder's post, David is depicted as a great young and mature man who is even thinking about possibly being a pastor someday. I was thrilled to see such credit given to a young man of God. The interesting thing about the post was the number of times Wilder referenced David's maturity and actually called it an alternative lifestyle.

While the immediate context of Wilder's statement may have simply been a contrast between David and the other dudes who rip up the half-pipe, it does raise a question about what manhood really looks like in America and the post-modern West.

The sad reality is that a young man in his early 20s who is already married with children and a focused life used to be called normal in Western culture. Such is not always the case today. In fact, Kay Hymowitz ran a report in the *Wall Street Journal* a few years ago that posed the question, "Where Have the Good Men Gone?" In her article, Hymowitz observes that the Western culture is undergoing a phenomenon of dropout men of enormous proportions.[1] The truth of the matter is that countless boys and young men in America are clueless about what it means to be a man. So many of them are lost with nowhere to go and little reason to get there.

What does it really mean to be a man anymore? Are there answers? Does God have anything to say on the issue? Does it even matter? Where do we look for answers? Unlike other cultures in the world such as the Masi in Kenya, our present American and Western culture offers little real clues about manhood beyond the Hollywood celebrity who happens to currently be in the spotlight. The Masi, on the other hand, are required to go out on lion hunts and other similar experiences before they are considered men. And when they do come back, it's settled, and everyone knows they've crossed over a sacred bridge. What do we have? A driver's license? High school graduation? So what? Girls get those, too.

It Starts with the Boy

In unpacking this problem of manhood, we essentially have to go all the way back to boyhood. In the very beginning, we were created uniquely as separate females and males (Gen. 1:27). But the bottom line is that the human genetic code still exists as female and male. Boys and girls are different in the deepest parts of who they are. The problem is that we don't always allow boys, well, to be boys. One illustration of this is how our public schools are organized. Many times, the systems hinder the total development of young boys.

A while back, the *Washington Post* ran a great article by Jennifer Fink called "Why Schools Are Failing Our Boys."[2] Fink described getting e-mails from her son's teacher who was worried about how he couldn't sit still and how he lacked any desire to cooperate with the system. The clarification of the problem came when Jennifer connected the dots that, because it was winter, her son was confined inside all day and therefore restless. At home, he was allowed to bundle up and go outside to burn energy, which he did. But the school system was afraid that he and all the other children might get sick playing in the cold and confined them inside with no real outlet for his God-given energy.

I got a chuckle as I read Jennifer's post, not only because I agreed with her but because I lived it. Remember that whole first-grade drama—both years of it? Boys generally are different from girls. We have to work with them differently and expect them to act differently. If boys are not allowed to fully nurture their masculinity as children, they will struggle with it as they grow into adult men. When a boy feels the urge to see explosions and attack something, give them an axe and some firewood instead of labeling them poor students and setting them up for failure.

The Honor of Masculinity

In Ephesians 5:33, Paul lovingly urges wives to respect their husbands. Not only do we see many in our day balking at the idea of a wife honoring and respecting her husband, but the media often encourages the opposite. TV shows, movies, and jokes in the lunchroom are filled with pictures of men portrayed as idiots, sloths, or criminals. The idea of a man being noble or honorable and worthy of respect is almost a lost art form and sometimes even shunned. Those who discount this principle of a wife honoring her husband rarely have a problem with the preceding section where husbands are exhorted to love their wives in the same way that Christ loves the church. And how is it that Christ loves the church? He died violently for the church.

Deep within the masculine soul is a desire to protect and make the hard self-sacrifices for others. The interesting thing about men and depression is that despondency occurs more often with guys who feel they are not needed than with men who feel they are making a difference for others. When was the last time we told a man that we appreciate his hard work and sacrifice for others? Those simple words might be the first steps in honoring dads and men in our lives.

The Encouraging Call to Manhood

It was late November 1996 when we returned from the mission field to move to our first full-time ministry. The process included renting a moving truck and car trailer in tow. I had never driven anything that big before, and I was a bit concerned, especially with the car trailer attached. My dad never taught me how to handle anything that big. Actually, he never really encouraged me to do anything bigger than my present reality.

But my friend Todd, who is now a Bible translator in Papua New Guinea, was with me as we made the final connections for the taillights. We wiped our hands off and took a deep breath from a job well-done. Then, after another deep breath, I said, "Todd, you know, I've never really driven anything this big before, and honestly I'm a bit afraid that I'm going to wreck it or something." Todd just looked at me and nodded his head once with a small smile. I went on, "But I guess I just need to be a man about it and push forward." Again, Todd just gave a small smile and quick nod and only offered a one-word response: "Yup."

That's really all there was to it from then on. We prayed, asking for God's help. I then shook Todd's hand, thanked him, climbed into the cab, and took off. But that's what I needed. I needed another guy to tell me that I was a man and that I could do it.

I know I'm not alone in this search. I know it's been this way before. Way back in the first century, the apostle Paul exhorted men to "be watchful, stand firm in the faith, *act like men*, be strong. Let all that you do be done in love" (emphasis added) (1 Cor. 16:13–14 ESV). As I read those verses, I can't help but imagine how different life would be if men would fully rise up to live that kind of life. When men actually rise up and take responsibility for themselves and make sacrifices for others, only good can come from such a culture. Maleness is something we are born with, but it's in working out that masculinity that men are produced. That's why we need men like Paul and Todd and others who have journeyed with God and are able to point the way for boys and young men.

I mentioned Marked Men for Christ earlier, and I honestly can't think of a better ministry for men today. Sure, there are a lot of great men's events. But the key to Marked Men for Christ is its continued strategy of brotherhood. Beyond the initial weekend event where guys are challenged to remove their facades, the ministry calls them to step into life with one another like a platoon of Marines willing to take shrapnel for others. It's that iron-sharpens-iron design that Solomon spoke about in Proverbs 27:17. Men need other men in their lives, which is especially true for guys who grew up without dads. It sure has been true for me.

As noted, I lived part of my childhood without a dad in the house. During those seasons, my mother tried to include some men in my life, men such as my uncle who walked with God. She didn't fret over getting more ladies into my impressionable heart. She knew that men and women are different and that I needed the gift of masculinity and the challenge of manhood. Today, there are times when I meet a young boy and extend my hand, but instead of offering a high five, I'll say something like, "Let's shake hands like men." Sometimes it's those little encouragements along the way that help a boy realize who he is and what he can become someday, no matter what his personal temperament might be. He just needs to hear—from a man—that he indeed is or will be a man someday.

I still remember one of those transformational steps. It wasn't big, but it was recognition, and sometimes that's enough to get the ball rolling. We were at my aunt and uncle's house for some kind of family gathering, and I was the only kid my age there. I was in the dining area, bored out of my skull listening to my mom, aunt, and three or four other ladies talk. Then, I heard my uncle's father yell at me from the back patio: "Steve, what are you doing? Come out here and sit with the men." It was a little thing, but why do I remember it still to this day? Because a man I respected called me out to be with him. If this man was calling me a man, then possibly I'd be a man someday, too. Thus I am.

CHAPTER 5

CHICK-FIL-A, CORSETS, AND GOD ON SEX

If God's got anything better than sex to offer,
he's certainly keeping it to himself.

—Sting

May your fountain be blessed, and may you rejoice in the wife
of your youth. . . . How beautiful you are and how pleasing,
my love, with your delights!

—Solomon

It had been a long day when Deb and I dropped off our girls for youth group. We try to grab date nights whenever we can. When you've been married for 27 years, even fast food has a romantic ring to it. So with a coupon from one of Deb's students, we headed to Chick-fil-A with the anticipation of not having to clean a kitchen and enjoying some time without teen drama. The problem was that the line was taking forever, and the day was just getting longer.

I wanted to bolt, but Deb was much more patient. To encourage me, she suggested a bet, something she hardly ever does. In her confidence, she wagered that if we were not through the line in 10 minutes, she'd wear a corset that night.

What? A preacher talking about the intimate details in marriage? Well, why not? When you think about it, the Bible speaks about the subject in quite wonderful ways. The unfortunate reality is that our present Western culture has allowed Hollywood to highjack the subject. Thus, life has been permeated with myths that ultimately lead to a whole lot of pain. I've experienced some of it. Consider these five fake truths on the subject:

Myth #1: God is down on sex. That lie suggests that there is segregation of good sex and Christianity, church, or deep Bible study. "Good Christian boys and girls don't talk about sex" is what this myth says.

Myth #2: Sex in the context of Christian marriage is boring. This myth suggests that the real fun is outside the bonds of biblical Christianity. The myth says that God's way is restrictive. After all, God's down on fun.

Myth #3: Everyone is doing it before marriage. Yes, we live in a culture that is permeated by premarital sex, but the truth is that not everyone is doing it. There really are those who wait until marriage for sex, which is something the Hollywood hype ignores or makes fun of.

Myth #4: It's just physical. Ask any woman or man the night after a passionate hookup or a sexual relationship that has just come to an end. They will tell you that there is an undeniable and unquantifiable void left after the act that has deep roots in the soul.

Myth #5: Premarital sex helps discern compatibility. The truth is that veteran married couples doing it God's way actually experience their best sex years in the marriage commitment.

The Maker of Sex
If Hollywood is wrong, and if we are more than accidents of evolutionary chance, then the assumption is that God is the ultimate maker of sex. Genesis 1:27–28 clearly teaches that God intended

humans to multiply, but what may surprise many is that God's design is much more than biological reproduction. In fact, Solomon, the wisest man who has ever lived, painted a picture of marital sex that is far beyond mere procreation and rather quite exciting. Two scripture passages to consider are Song of Solomon 7:1–9 and Proverbs 5:18–19. In addition, it's amazing to look at the first marriage in Genesis 2:19–25 and see a sexual relationship before brokenness entered the picture: a man and a woman who were naked without shame. In other words, when sex was done the designer's way, there was no drama, heartache, dysfunction, or regret. It was good beyond the momentary euphoria.

Yup, what God has created in sex really is a beautiful thing when expressed in its proper boundaries. It's something that Hollywood totally misses out on but the church can quite possibly restore.

Oh yes, the Chick-fil-A line. Well, I have to report that they lived up to their promise and Deb's expectation. We did get our food within the 10-minute bet parameters. But I sure did keep my foot on the brake as long as I could. "Sir, yes, you really do pick up your food at the second window."

Finding Grace and Following the Guide

When Deb and I got married, she was a virgin and I was not. One of the modern myths about sex is that it's just physical and no big deal. I don't believe that, and it is certainly not my experience. My emotions have been all over the place in my adult life. At one point, I can experience the true forgiveness and redemption of Jesus with an understanding of grace that people with less checkered lives just can't understand. On the other hand, there are still residual times when I ache over my premarital sexual activity. I don't blame the girls. I know it was my decision, and it pains me. If there were anything I could take back, it would be the premarital sex during the dark ages of my high school years and young adult life. But I can't.

Regardless of what culture says, the Bible is very clear that God not only made sex beautiful, but he also made it for marriage. The original divine design for sexuality was in the exclusive relationship between one man and one woman for life. Jesus went back to creation in Mark 10:6–8 to define the relationship. Does the Bible mention polygamy as some critics of Christianity claim? Yes, but that was never God's design. The ancient order was one man and one woman in which intimacy could flourish. The author of Hebrews exhorted the first Christians to purity of the marriage bed and noted that judgment would come to those who ignored God's design. As Solomon beautifully pictured the glory of married sexuality, he also cautioned against the pain of stepping outside of God's design. Note Proverbs 7:22–23 and 6:26–28. Today, we can see that damage all around us in the form of emotional baggage, dysfunction, and distrust.

So, what do we do when we blow it? In short, we confess our sin, accept God's grace, and move forward. But it may take time to fully experience his grace and incorporate it into your soul. It did for me.

A few years ago, I was aggressively studying men's ministry issues and attended a conference led by John Eldredge. At first, I hated it. I had expected a more experiential and hands-on event, like the ministry of Marked Men for Christ. What I got was an enormous group of about 800 men in an auditorium listening to lectures by Eldredge and his team. After the Thursday night opening session, I called three of my close mentor friends to rant about my experience. These were guys who knew where I was, both geographically and emotionally. Lately, I'd been trekking some of this journey with them, and all three seemed to be on the same wavelength. In short, they all basically gave me the same answer: "Be still, Steve." One told me to find a seat on the front row for the rest of the three-and-a-half-day event. I wanted to rip his head off. But trying to have an attitude of submission to my elder brothers and an open heart to God, I got up very early the next morning, went to the dark auditorium, and set my notebook on the third seat from the center, front row, just about 10 feet from the main lectern.

The breakthrough came later when Eldredge was speaking on men, women, and sexuality. Much of it dealt with the problem of so many guys today looking to the beautiful maiden to find their self-worth. You can't do that. A woman may acknowledge a man's power, but to find meaning, a man must turn to other men and, more importantly, to God. The point of connection, though, was when Eldredge told a story about one of his girlfriends who became pregnant before he was a Christian. I remembered reading about this in his book, *Wild at Heart*. The girl had an abortion with Eldredge's approval, and years later, he felt the sting and sorrow of those events. But then the change came. He masterfully described the transformation of his repentance, accepting the grace of Christ, and then fully releasing his sin into the hands of Jesus. He had to let the sin go. It was after this full release that he was able to move forward.

Immediately after the lecture, I quickly jumped right up in front of him. Remember, my friend made me sit on the front row. I reached out to Eldredge and asked, "That story in your book, about your old girlfriend having an abortion, was that true?"

"Yes," he said with a serious though compassionate look on his face.

"You really were able to eventually release it all to Jesus and go forward?"

"Yes."

"So somehow, I have to do the same thing."

"Yes."

I don't remember much of the conversation after that, but I do remember that it was, indeed, a real turning point. I had been through similar conversations with God before, but this time, it seemed more real. Here was a guy, just a guy, who had truly blown it, but he had also truly experienced the grace of Jesus and could now help others.

Today, I am reminded of that exchange and often return to it since Satan has a way of bringing up my past again and again. Being reminded that Jesus took my sin on the cross and granted me grace helps me look forward.

Looking forward is what we need to do—no, get to do—once we confess our sin and receive God's grace. Going forward is not just living in peace; it is deliberately choosing Jesus over sin. I'm often reminded of John 8 where Jesus extended his grace to a woman caught in adultery. The text is speculative since it is not found in the oldest manuscripts that are closest to the actual words of Christ. But the narrative fits. When people want to condemn judgments of morality, they often point to this text where Jesus refuses to condemn the woman. What they most often leave off, though, are the final words of Christ in which he exhorts her to leave her life of sin. Jesus called her not only to accept his grace but to live differently from that moment on.

That's the call for you and me. Yes, sex is a beautiful thing that God blessed humanity with. But it gets ugly really fast when we take it out of his loving context. The reason I talk about these delicate issues is not because I want to be self-righteous or judgmental. I just want to spare others the pain. I touched the hot burner, and I hope I can prevent others from doing the same.

Have you blown it sexually? God knows all about it, and he longs to bring healing and a new start. That's the whole reason Jesus died on the cross and rose from the grave. No matter the sin, Jesus paid for it. When we approach the cross of Christ, he extends his grace and makes it possible for us to live a new life no matter where we've been or what we've done. Today, I have a new life because of his grace, and I'm following the designer's old but true guide for sexuality. That's what I've experienced, and I pray you can, too.

Jesus on Marriage

If Jesus spoke on grace and forgiveness in regard to sexual sin in general, what did he say about marriage in particular? A couple of years ago, Chick-fil-A fell under LGBT and social scrutiny because its founder, S. Truett Cathy, openly declared his position on what many describe as traditional marriage, the principle of one man and one woman for life. Some businesses, organizations, and civic groups boycotted the franchise. This is America, and if those groups want to protest and boycott, it is their right as long as they refrain from violence. The question, though, is not about politics or governance, but about God. What does God say about it?

I have friends who say that Jesus never spoke on the issue of gay marriage. Therefore, the reasoning goes, if Jesus never spoke on the issue and certainly didn't condemn gay marriage, then it must be fine. If we're looking for those specific words—*gay marriage*—then maybe they are correct. But there are other issues—embezzlement, for example—that Jesus never talked about either. Yet we know where Jesus stands because of what he said in general about possessions: "Give back to Caesar what is Caesar's and to God what is God's" (Mark 12:17), among other references. In the same way, we can see that Jesus covered not only the idea of gay marriage but all marital issues when he took the religious debaters of his day all the way back to Genesis.

God created humans distinctly as male and female, the two being differently and completely complementary to each other. Marriage is the union of two different beings into one. From passages such as Proverbs 5:18–19 and Song of Solomon 7:1–9, it's clear that God also created sex for marriage and that it is a beautiful union in its proper context.

More problems arise, however, when we move further and further away from God's design. In Mark 10:2–9, Jesus spoke on the origins of marriage and thus its intent by God. When looking at the immediate context, the religious zealots were not focused on getting as close as possible to the heart of God but rather how close to the edge of sin they could get without falling off the cliff. Specifically, they were debating how lax one could be about divorce while still having God's favor.

In response, Jesus reminded them that marriage is not a mere legal contract but rather a divine institution designed by God. Their problem was their hearts and attitudes toward the institution. For them, it was not a matter of living out the ideal of God; it was about negotiating human sin. The divine plan was lost to human preference, and people suffered just as they do today.

The present cultural debate really began by separating sex from marriage. Beliefs changed from a commitment to marriage first and sex second. When our propensities, feelings, and emotions rule, we no longer pursue God's best but fit God into our best. When we step back and really listen to Jesus, we find that sex and marriage were all God's idea in the first place, and they were good in God's original creation.

When it comes to this debate on gay marriage, my thoughts have changed some. The change is not one of surrendering clear biblical teaching, but rather understanding better the heart of those who struggle with this issue. The truth is that some people honestly wrestle with homosexual feelings and propensities. To simply say "Stop feeling that way" is about as helpful as simply telling a man who wrestles with adulterous heterosexual feelings to, well, "feel something different." It's doesn't work that way. Because our world is broken, our feelings can also be broken. So the answer is much deeper. In any broken society, the closer we pursue God's design, the closer we come to our own healing. The more we pursue Jesus, the more we can see marriage and sexuality as truly good. But we are not without help. Here are six challenges to help us move closer to God's design, no matter where we are along the path.

1. *Hold to truth.*

When it comes to morality and spirituality, truth today is often defined in the eye of the beholder. If it feels good to you, it must be right for you. Because of that, sometimes we fear holding the line on areas that may offend others, and we surrender divine absolutes out of fear of cultural backlash. But Jesus never walked that path. While Christ came to love in the most profound and sacrificial way possible, he also came with truth and grace. Although culturally acceptable sins will vary through the ages, the truth of God remains consistent and unmoved by the winds of political pressure.

2. *Respond in love.*

Sometimes, Christ-followers hold up righteousness while offering no grace at all. "Jerks for Jesus" is what I like to call those who make it their life's ambition to tell others how wrong they are while stroking their own self-righteous egos. While Jesus and the Bible do speak of absolute truth, Paul reminded the first believers and us today that we are to *"do everything in love"* (1 Cor. 16:14). It's possible to confidently stand for something without being mean in the process. We can demonstrate love by our tone and actions toward those around us whether or not we agree with them.

3. *Empathize with others.*

Those who long for gay marriage often feel a genuine propensity toward people of the same sex. Sometimes, it's because of wounds or dysfunctions from their childhood, and sometimes, there may really be no explanation for it. In the same way a person may wrestle with heterosexual temptation, a person may also wrestle with homosexual temptation. The Bible is clear that the sin is not in the root emotion or propensity but in the action. I've often found that many times we are much more generous with our own struggles than we are with others' struggles.

4. Look in the mirror.

When tempted to bring down the gauntlet of judgment, remind yourself that Jesus warned his followers to examine their own lives first. He even approached it with a bit of dry humor, noting that we should take the plank out of our own eye before grasping at the splinter in someone else's. We may not wrestle with homosexual temptation, but we need to be honest about our own struggles and spend more time drawing our hearts toward Christ rather than criticizing others.

5. Extend grace with a call for repentance.

For quite some time, I've heard people reference Jesus's compassion to the woman caught in adultery. That is certainly a beautiful illustration of the heart of Christ. Jesus also suggests that condemnation and execution come from the one without sin. The religious zealots got the point and walked away with their heads down. But that's where people stop. They want to remove all divine boundaries and stop just shy of the part where Jesus also exhorts the woman to *"leave your life of sin"* (John 8:11). Likewise, in John 4, Jesus never excuses the sin of the woman who was living with a man after multiple broken marriages, but he does offer her grace and a new life to the fullest. We can only experience the complete riches of grace when we admit our need for it.

6. Honor the institution.

Debi and I just celebrated our 27th wedding anniversary. Bless Deb's heart for putting up with me so long. Recently, a woman commented on the novelty of a 27-year marriage. Many young people experiment with sex early and get married late, if at all, because we've been hurt and have hurt others. Marriage is viewed as an ancient relic of our grandparents but not necessary or desirable for today. The media assume that lifelong marriage is out of style, and most of our modern enlightened culture marches to this tune. But it doesn't have to be that way. In fact, Jesus promised that it can be quite the opposite.

I've not been the perfect husband, and I can easily point to my library of mistakes in our marriage. There are countless actions and words I wish I could do over in the right way. But that's the thing about Jesus; he knows what I've done and still loves me anyway. He died for my sin and rose from the grave, signifying that his death was enough to pay for my penalty. But he also came to give new life and new direction. That new direction is available for all of us. It's true for us as individuals in our own story and also as we look at the institution of marriage itself. We may be swimming upstream, but the kingdom view of sexuality and marriage is something that can bring healing and hope to a broken and hurting world. By the way we talk and act toward marriage, we can point the world back to God's plan and God's glory in marriage. It worked for Adam and Eve before sin entered the picture, and it can work again for us today.

Managing Sex

Songs and movies speak of sex as making love, and that phrase might not be too far off. Like in any other facet of human relationships, sex takes work, and the best sex doesn't usually come until after a few years of marriage. The key is to focus on the other person's needs, making their needs and desires your priority (see 1 Cor. 7:3–5). Sex isn't about what feels good but about what is good, making beautiful sex for the other person. The beauty comes when we focus on what glorifies God and what gratifies your spouse.

The result is joy. In premarital counseling, I explain that when a couple says no to everyone else (forsaking all others), they are giving a full and hearty yes to each other. Indeed, God gives a healthy and hearty yes to sex. It's amazing that despite all the screw-ups in my high school and junior college years, God still found a place for me in this realm. For you, no matter where you've been and no matter what you've done, Jesus still offers you that same healing and a fresh start. There's a whole lot of hope in that.

CHAPTER 6
PONDERING POLITICS AND PIETY

*Politics is almost as exciting as war, and quite as dangerous.
In war, you can only get killed once, but in politics many times.*

—Winston Churchill

My kingdom is not of this world.

—Jesus Christ

I've always enjoyed watching national and international news, but not so much local news. My mother and extended relatives marveled over me as a preschooler sitting with the adults, seriously paying attention to what was going on. Today, names like Walter Cronkite, Barbara Walters, and Tom Brokaw all mean something to me. I know those names because I was with them in the imagination of a young boy. Beyond US politics, I was always mesmerized by other countries. One of my grandmothers picked up on this and set me up with a subscription to *National Geographic*. Come to think of it, I think I still have about 20 old editions in a storage box someplace.

Wherever the action was, that's where I wanted to be. I wanted to know what was going on, even if I didn't understand the complexities and all the details of politics, governance, and finance. Prior to first grade, I once debated with my mother about the US dollar.

I suggested that the government should simply print more currency, and my mom didn't agree. Maybe I should have been a politician.

Today, life is different, and I don't pay much attention to politics anymore. At least I try not to. It's somewhat dangerous and unhealthy for me. I can't remember the last time I actually sat down to watch the evening news or a midday program on CNN, FOX, or another network. But no matter how hard I try, the news continues to creep into my life like an unwanted contagion—the radio, social media, conversations with friends. Facebook and other social media can be the worst. I went off of Facebook for a few years and then realized that venues like that can be a valuable tool to share a positive message and most certainly the love of Christ with the world.

Facebook can also be a device to steal my day and my heart. There are a lot of issues in the nation and the world that I care about. There are pains and philosophies that lead to pain. My heart pushes me to cry out for justice, longing to make things right. But where do God, faith, and country intersect? That's been a hard question to try to answer over the past 10 years or so. Some days, I can't get my head or heart out of the media because of what some politician or political activist is doing, and I desperately want to help them all.

I have friends all over the place on the issue. By this, I'm not talking about any specific political or social issue but rather the way a follower of Jesus should respond to government. My friend Joe, who helped me pass Greek in college, is now a constitutional law attorney and has spent a number of years defending Christians in cases on freedom of religion. He's good at what he does. Then I've got other friends who believe that because we are part of the eternal kingdom of heaven, entering into politics or social justice is a waste of time and a total distraction. As in many issues, there is a balance. Paul exhorted Timothy to keep his head in all situations, and *balance* may, indeed, be the right word here.

The Founding Fathers

Part of my tension essentially comes from the freedom I have as an American citizen. In this country, anyone can participate in the political process, and that's a good thing. But this truth is somewhat muddied today because of modern misunderstandings of the Establishment Clause in the First Amendment. The First Amendment was a reaction to the British Empire's mandate that everyone submit to the Church of England. Even now, the British pay part of their taxes to the church. America's founding fathers didn't want to make the same mistake. However, their intent was not to totally eliminate God from government or the public sector.

Politicians today misunderstand what it means to separate church from state. They say it's okay to talk about God at home, church, and any other place except your job and certainly not in government. But the truth is that if God is, indeed, real, then he has wisdom for every aspect of our lives. That includes everything and everyone, whether he or she is a plumber, plastic surgeon, preacher, or president.

One illustration of this is William Wilberforce, a leader of the movement to stop slave trade in England. That was years before the American Civil War, a fight over a state's right to secede. But the big powder keg that led to the war was the debate over slavery. Slavery in the United States finally came to an end through Lincoln's Emancipation Proclamation and after the deaths of hundreds of thousands of young men. But long before that, across the Atlantic Ocean, a conscientious, religious man—William Wilberforce—spent years in the British Parliament working for the abolition of slavery. He eventually won the battle without a single gunshot.

Like Wilberforce, I bring my faith into every area of my life, all the way down to picking up trash, pursuing ethical business practices, and voting on decisions made in the Oval Office. A more authentic Christianity would be a good thing for everyone. Look at it this way. A major tenet of Christianity is this: *"Greater love has no one than this:*

to lay down one's life for one's friends" (John 15:13). That totally goes against the grain of our modern me-and-my-rights society. Christ taught us to deny ourselves for others. Can you think of anything better for a society than an environment in which everyone looks solely to the interests of others rather than themselves?

That doesn't mean I'm advocating a new political party or championing an existing one. I'm certainly not saying that Christ-followers should act like jerks and cram their agendas down the throats of those who don't agree with them. But I am saying that we cannot dichotomize between politics and religion. Real faith is something that intersects every aspect of life, and it follows that as everyone lives out his or her God-given call, many people will experience the love of Christ.

The Father

The Constitution does afford me the right to participate in religion as long as I don't demand a national religion or veto the right of others who believe differently. But what about the higher authority? What about God and the Bible?

What's clear from Romans 13 is that God creates governments and deposes them, for government brings order to society. Think of traffic laws. With no system or societal order, chaos would ensue. From there, God calls Christians to submit to the government unless those in authority call us to sin against him. This is illustrated in passages such as Acts 4:19–20, in which Peter and John refuse the Sanhedrin's demand that they cease preaching in the name of Jesus.

The Bible also calls Christians to pray for those in authority. But beyond that, the text doesn't say much. Therefore, those living in Western democracies are free to participate in the process of government as long as they do not sin. Some people may be called into public government service. If that is the case, then they are to work at it with all their hearts and struggle with maintaining the right motives. Paul challenged the Colossian Christians to work at *"whatever you do with all your heart, as working for the Lord, not for human masters"* (Col. 3:23).

The Last Will and Testament of a Young Republican

That's right, I was once a Young Republican—my senior year in high school, to be exact. I didn't go to too many meetings before I moved on to another adventure, but I believed what these folks stood for, at least what little I knew at the time. But things are different now, and it has nothing to do with my age. Now, before my lefty friends get all excited, you need to know that I'm not defecting to your political party, either. I'm pressing the cancel button on the whole system as far as my involvement goes. While this doesn't mean I'm never going to vote on issues I believe in, it does mean a drastic and purposeful decision to refrain from direct political party support and involvement. Even on my Facebook page, I've declared the kingdom of heaven as my political view. We're part of the eternal kingdom, which supersedes the greatest kingdoms of humankind.

This is a freedom issue, for all must work out their present calling. For me, I've had to set some boundaries. In wrestling with this for years, I had at least three realizations that bolstered my decision to pull the plug on political parties. These discoveries have saved me, or they have at least set me on a healthier road.

1. Political parties are incomplete.

While I tend to lean toward conservative Republican, neither major political party has it all right. They both have some huge things going for them, but neither one really possesses a corner on the market of truth. A big issue for me is the sanctity of life, which sits well with Republicans and their anti-abortion platform. But Democrats tend to defend the rights of the little guy, the poor, which is something the Bible also speaks about. So to claim allegiance to one party over another is to ignore issues that are biblical and endorsed by the other side.

2. Political parties are divisive.

This is an easy one to see from my perspective, for I have friends on both sides of the political arena who claim allegiance first to Christ. The problem is that we often get hot and bothered by particular legislations and build walls against each other that eventually turn into stone-throwing. I like what one guy said a while back, that most often Republicans paint all Democrats as being morally corrupt and loose, while Democrats position all Republicans as ignorant fools with unprogressive thinking. As a preacher for the kingdom of God, I run the risk of alienating people who need the love of Christ when I harp on issues that are not eternal. While I may believe that I'm logically right on some of these political issues, they are minimal in light of lost souls and eternity.

3. Political parties are too tempting for me.

I can easily get carried away and miss the big picture and the point. I can lose focus and miss or blow a chance to convey what is eternal and really important. So I try to bite my tongue and refocus as much as I can in order to stay on track. I suppose it would be similar to a recovering alcoholic staying clear of a bar. It's just not worth it.

The Bigger Answer

I'm not saying that all Christians are to stay out of politics. Scripture doesn't forbid it. Wilberforce illustrates that so well. There have been brilliant apologists—Justin Martyr, Clement of Alexandria, and Augustine—who spoke of the truths, benefits, and hopes of Christ and his followers. The problem occurs when Christ-followers put all their eggs in the basket of legal action and forget to actually follow Christ. I wonder if we've forgotten that Jesus came first to seek and to save individual souls, not the culture at large. When a heart is changed, the hands will follow. The first followers of Christ were salt and light in their communities and governments. The testimonies of their daily lives ultimately turned the Roman Empire upside down.

Politics and a Buffet-Line Jesus

I made a clear line in the sand about my government involvement, but there are still times when the political bug jumps up and bites me. In those times, I almost want to yell into the air as Jesus did when Peter was trying to derail the master's mission. Jesus commanded, *"Get behind me, Satan!"* (Matt. 16:23). The past six months have been one of those seasons.

For some time, many Christian leaders have rightly pointed out the negative divisiveness that occurs when Christ-followers trumpet social issues above Christ in the world. Subjects such as gay marriage and abortion are particularly illustrative. There's a fine balance between simply getting the word out and bombardment. I've probably done some bombardment at times, and I'm sorry for that.

Some Christians speak truth without love, and we must give them caution. I'm frustrated over the growing number of Christ-followers who come from social left environments to now play what the so-called religious right is guilty of. I've seen many of them quoting God to prove their political platforms. Some people who never talk about God are now quoting scripture in social media as though they have a PhD in theology in order to demonstrate all the ways their political opponents are wrong. Large groups of evangelicals have united in sending petitions to the Oval Office about immigration. I know preachers who have dedicated entire Sunday sermons to social issues, and one pastor even chided others for not following suit. News journals, which normally are skeptical about Jesus, have started running articles on what they believe God thinks about healthcare.

Many who scream the loudest that God is on their side criticized the political right for doing the very same thing six months ago. So

67

which is it? Is one side of the social political debate on or off limits? Are not both really just as divisive to the true cause of Christ? Can we just pick and choose? It's like a cheap buffet. You go through the line, pick what you like, and pass by the rest.

Many American Christians do this with Jesus. Instead of submitting all their thinking to Jesus, they pick and choose what most closely aligns with their preferences and ignore anything that contradicts their chosen worldview. How can a Christian find the healthy ground? How can we live first as kingdom citizens and still walk with a love for our country and the people we disagree with?

To pursue political change, here are some questions to ask ourselves:

1. Am I honestly examining both sides of the question?

If you're going to quote Jesus as an authority on one issue, be sure to lift him up on the others that you may not necessarily care about or even like. One problem with the majority of media outlets is that they are clearly governed by either a left or right political agenda. Unbiased journalism is a rarity today. If we're truly attempting to live like Christ, it's imperative that we step out of our comfort zones and listen attentively and humbly to all sides of the narrative.

2. Am I making my issue their issue?

Because of some wounds in my early years, I've always had a heart for family social issues. I tend to speak more about pro-life and a biblical understanding of marriage. Those are personal for me, but they are not as personal for others, and there is the rub. We all have issues that, for whatever reason, are hot buttons for us and not for others. For that reason, we can't just assume our social issues are a mandate by God for everyone. The range of potential social topics is as wide as the Pacific Ocean. You just can't cover them all. A short list of some of those hot buttons include abortion, marriage, refugees, world hunger, homeschooling, public education, all-natural foods, vaccinations, gun control, environment, dress, entertainment, and alcohol. The list continues. One or many of those issues may have a strong place in your heart. If so, then do what you can to bring healing and answers, but that does not necessarily mean it's God's individual calling for everyone.

3. Am I focusing on the big picture?

The first church in the Bible was predominantly Hebrew. It's easy to see some possible tension when a vast number of Greek Gentile believers began accepting Christ. Two cultures and customs were colliding like runaway freight trains on the same track heading toward each other. What's interesting is that the apostles recognized that in Acts 15, and under the Holy Spirit's direction, they did not require the Hebrew Law of Moses to be kept by the new Gentile Christians. The focus was solely on Christ. Likewise, are we holding up issues that steer us away from the centrality of Jesus and his restoration? It's quite possible to force legislation toward our own passions but never fail to change the human heart.

4. Am I really helping or just yelling?

It's one thing to talk the talk and quite another to walk the walk. In politics, it's easy to vote for government assistance and quite another thing to reach into our own pockets to help the poor. It's easy to talk about supporting pro-life legislation and another to actually sacrifice money and time to support crisis pregnancy ministries.

5. Am I acting and speaking in love or arrogance?

There is truth to some issues. However, the Bible clearly teaches us to speak the truth in love. If our attitude or tone projects any arrogance or self-righteousness, then it's better to keep quiet. We may win a battle but still lose an eternal life through our misdirected agenda.

6. Am I spending more time in God's word than in social and news media?

There's probably no need for commentary here. The easiest way to live out the kingdom of God is to spend more time in God's word than the world's word. By a systematic reading through the Bible, the Holy Spirit will change us and help us see more sides to the issue and how Jesus would act and react in our present culture.

A Changed Heart

Government-run healthcare is a hot debate. Some want to keep a strong, mandatory government program in place and even expand it. Others fear it. But one of the real, underlying issues here is greed, which more laws just can't fix. When we moved to the northwest Houston area, we needed to find a family doctor. A week later, I was in a new building with sick people, filling out forms. I try to leave as many blank lines as possible. The nurse on the other side of the window never asked me why I wanted to see the doctor, but she sure wanted to know who my insurance company was. It all came down to money, and that's an issue that no law can change.

The deeper issues facing the United States or any country cannot be solved by politics, no matter how good they are. The answer is found only in a changed heart, and only Jesus can change hearts. When people are transformed on the inside, they desire to do right whether there is a law mandating it or not. That's where the ultimate answer rests—the love of Jesus Christ that will change a life and a nation.

CHAPTER 7
HOPE WHEN ALL THE LIGHTS GO OUT

Lord, my God, who am I that You should forsake me?
I am told God loves me—and yet the reality of darkness & coldness
& emptiness is so great that nothing touches my soul.

—Mother Teresa, 1957

It is said that in some countries trees will grow,
but will bear no fruit, because there is no winter there.

—John Bunyan

Hope is patience with the lamp lit.

—Tertullian

The kids had long been asleep, and Debi had just dozed off. I was staring at the ceiling. I remember thinking that if a guy like me wanted to end it all, the easiest way to do it was to take every bottle of ibuprofen in the house and just go to sleep. All the baggage and brokenness of the past few years had escalated to a crescendo, and I simply didn't see any good coming out of anything in my life.

I once heard a famous radio preacher talk about suicide, and he made the comment that those who take such a route are making an utterly cowardly decision. It wasn't just his statement that bothered me; it was the arrogance in his voice, that he was somewhat better than those weak and pitiful people. Don't get me wrong. Suicide is terrible. It is evil. But what this high-powered homiletician couldn't understand is that sometimes the people who have committed this wretched act didn't do so out of cowardice but rather from a disturbed spirit that told them what they were doing would be good for others. Why do I say that? Because I was almost there. I felt like a failure, and because of my failure, I couldn't do anything good for my spouse or those around me.

In that moment of darkness, my sick soul was telling me that Deb might actually be better off without me. The darkness didn't last long, and the thought that changed my emotional direction was that my kids needed a dad. That is probably what kept me going during that season. It's a dark place that not everyone experiences. Sure, we all get down at times, but clinical depression is another story.

It's surprising the number of great leaders who've walked through this valley. Martin Luther suffered depression, and Winston Churchill openly admitted his struggle, referring to it as his black dog. The historical list is large and long and carries such names as John Adams, Mark Twain, Mozart, and Princess Diana. In a very dark season of Lincoln's life, he wrote a letter to his law partner, John Stuart, on January 23, 1841. It reads in part:

> I am now the most miserable man living. If what I feel were equally distributed to the whole human family, there would not be one cheerful face on the earth. Whether I shall ever be better I can not tell; I awfully forebode I shall not. To remain as I am is impossible; I must die or be better, it appears to me.[1]

One of the things I love about the Bible is its honesty. Both the prophet Elijah and the prophet Jeremiah felt suicidal at times. At one of the lowest points in Jeremiah's life, he cursed the day of his birth (Jer. 20:14, 18). While we don't know the specifics of the situation, the Sons of Korah cried out in Psalm 88:18, "Darkness is my closest friend." Whatever those biblical saints were feeling, I seemed to at least be in the same neighborhood with them that dark night.

One common denominator with many of those suffering depression is that they are passionate about life. I've experienced much empathetic sadness for others, especially those who don't know Jesus. That passion draws me to make great sacrifices in order to draw people to Jesus, but that passion can pull me into the pit. The two sides just seem to be connected, and it's only been through work and more time with Jesus that I've been able to find balance.

My depression didn't come from nowhere; it came from years of constant pressure now ready to explode. The real emotional pain began the last couple of years we were in California doing the church plant. Church planting can be very lonely at times, especially when you go into it without a team of friends around you. That's what we did, and I worked myself to the emotional bone. At one point, I saw a Christian counselor who told me that I was borderline clinically depressed. I felt alone in so many ways. Could things get worse?

Betrayal

There are certain days that stick in your mind. You live with them now like there is no distance between today and the real events. I'm writing this one day after the 16th anniversary of September 11, 2001. Nearly everyone who was past the age of 12 remembers where they were when they heard the news of the attack. Some older folks remember where they were when President John F. Kennedy was assassinated in Dallas in 1963. While Reagan survived his attack, I remember being in Mr. Watson's sixth-grade physical education class when he told us the news. We remember those tragic events that affected so many people.

I remember the day a trusted ministry colleague went back on his word about what I had believed was a divine opening and long-awaited answer to prayer. Three days earlier, after the other men left our men's Wednesday morning breakfast, Doug and I were talking about the future of the church we'd planted and my future dreams. We were five years into the project, and we were both tired. Most new churches don't last very long, and this is especially true of plants like ours without launch teams. But we were still going at it, ministering to people. We weren't big, and we were struggling financially. Doug and I sat there thinking about the future. Many times, we have to keep going in faith, for God's timeline is very rarely ours. You have to be faithful. You have to press forward. That is what we were doing, but we were just downright tired.

As we tried to figure out a direction, Doug suggested something that made me sit up straight. He knew the church was stuck and that my dreams were ultimately to start a church in the Dallas area, where I thought I'd be for the rest of my life. Doug knew that. He also felt like a change was needed in California—something to stir the waters.

So Doug reached out and said, "Let me see your plan, Steve. I'll help you work it out." Was this it? Was this the time I'd been praying about for years? Like a lion pouncing on a gazelle, I jumped. I told him I was ready to move on things—without praying about it or talking to my wife. Let me help you here. Not talking to your wife before making life-changing decisions is rarely a good idea.

But I had been working myself to death while keeping my real dream on the back burner, and this all made perfect sense. I pulled the trigger and began reaching out to friends and future ministry partners with the news. I couldn't have been more excited. Doug and I agreed to meet three days later to begin the initial steps of the project.

Then it happened. I drove a few miles down the road on Friday at the appointed time to meet Doug. He was already there waiting for me. Whatever small talk occurred, it wasn't much. Doug put his drink down on the table before me, took a breath, and said, "Steve, I don't believe you are entrepreneurial enough to pull this off. I'm not going to proceed in helping you with this." There was an immediate jolt and some back-and-forth conversation until I finally confessed, "Doug, I just feel raped by this." We had given everything to this cause. Physically, financially, spiritually, emotionally—we were all in. I had given everything, and now, after all this work and sacrifice, Doug had gone back on his word. His choice altered the course of my life.

Many of us have experienced some kind of betrayal. A business associate cancels a longstanding relationship for something new to put more cash in his own pocket. A spouse calls it quits on a marriage. A politician files away a promise in hopes no one will catch on.

We see many betrayals in the Bible. Joseph was sold into slavery by his brothers. A metal worker named Alexander harmed Paul and his associates. Judas betrayed Jesus—the ultimate betrayal.

Looking back at those biblical texts, sometimes we can see how God ultimately worked everything out for his purposes. Joseph wound up in Egypt and eventually became second in command to Pharaoh, gaining the power to make decisions that would eventually spare the future Hebrew nation from starvation. Jesus's death and resurrection made possible our salvation. We can often see God working in the lives of others. Whether he's working in our pain, well, that's another story.

Desert Tour

After leaving our church plant in California, I hit a number of bumps along the road. There were a few options that opened up for us, all of which I joyfully assumed were God's providential provision. But like my conversation with Doug, I saw them crumble in front of me for reasons I couldn't fathom.

We lived with relatives for a while—a complete humiliation for me. Eventually, I had to get some kind of job other than manual labor, and that's when my brother, who worked for a Christian college, called me. He told me about a church that was close to dying and needed a minister. So we packed up our kids and memories and moved to the northwest Houston area to jump in with a small church.

It was like a tugboat in the Galveston ship channel—cracks in the hold and taking on water incredibly fast. Don't get me wrong here. The people were nice and loving and took care of us. It's just that every single one of my ministry dreams had been crushed, and I felt like a complete failure. If my time in high school was the early dark ages of my life, this was probably the middle dark ages—really, a black hole is more like it.

Again, I want you to understand that the people in our church family were beautiful; they were not my problem. The problem was deeper. In a real sense, I not only felt betrayed by Doug, but by God as well. I'd made a choice to enter full-time ministry because I believed it was a calling. Ministry was not something I planned to get rich on. It was not for the benefits. I don't believe that God is a vending machine—you know, throw in some good deeds and then get rewarded. I believe in an intimate and personal relationship with God.

But in this season, I experienced profound wondering. I remember walking out of my house one afternoon and thinking about Jesus's words on God's love for his children in Matthew 7:7–11:

Ask and it will be given to you; seek and you will find; knock and the door will be opened to you. For everyone who asks receives; the one who seeks finds; and to the one who knocks, the door will be opened.

Which of you, if your son asks for bread, will give him a stone? Or if
he asks for a fish, will give him a snake? If you, then, though you are
evil, know how to give good gifts to your children, how much more
will your Father in heaven give good gifts to those who ask him!

As those words came to mind, I railed at God. I actually kicked
into the air and almost shouted, "Well, thanks, Jesus for the stone
and snake you just gave me!"

I suppose that's kind of how Elijah felt as well. Think about
it. Elijah and Jeremiah were 100 percent following God, but in the
eyes of the world, they seemed like failures. Maybe in their own
eyes, they also felt like failures at times.

My faith is no longer in the tank like it was back then, partly
because I'm reminding myself more often of what real faith is. There
are always those who claim that if you truly have faith, your life will
be a breeze, because obviously God wants you to be happy. But
that's not in the Bible.

When Faith Turns to Fatigue

Sometimes, we just get tired. If anything, the word *journey* better
describes the walk with Christ more than a happy stroll in the park.
It gets hard at times. It gets fatiguing. A marathon, or maybe a
triathlon, is more descriptive of what authentic Christianity is like,
not a Caribbean cruise. Yes, I get tired sometimes. It's tiring to pray
for years and not see the results my heart longs for. It's downright
oppressive to calmly and lovingly speak about biblical righteousness
in a culture that wholly embraces spiritual, moral, and philosophical
relativity. It's disheartening to see more and more people who wear
the name of Christ reject a biblical worldview in favor of liberal
cultural and political correctness.

It gets hard arguing for truth when others reject it for the lies of
Satan—lies that go all the way back to the Garden of Eden—"*Did*

God really say?" (Gen. 3:1). It's also frustrating to see Christians put on legalistic self-righteousness and flash it like a billboard, expecting to earn their way into heaven. By their arrogance, they not only damage their own souls but also the lost lives of those who watch them. I get tired when I think of all the times I've shared the love of Christ with people who ignored the grace they so desperately need.

It gets hard just doing life. It's hard to keep the faith while being a husband and dad and wondering how to provide for my wife and kids as I attempt another day of advancing the ball down the field. It's hard to keep the eyes of my heart on the big eternal picture when the eyes of my head see those who reject God, living what appears to be a successful lifestyle without a care in the world as they tread over the backs of those who love Jesus. It just gets hard sometimes.

We are not alone on our journey. Many have walked this path before us. I'm reminded of Asaph, who said this:

> *Surely in vain I have kept my heart pure and have washed my hands in innocence. All day long I have been afflicted, and every morning brings new punishments. . . . When I tried to understand all this, it troubled me deeply till I entered the sanctuary of God; then I understood their final destiny* (Ps. 73:13–14, 16–17).

Asaph was one of the leaders in David's choirs who, like so many of us, knew the drain of trying to live for God in a world that would rather not. As Asaph meditated in Psalm 73 on the condition of the culture around him, he felt like a defeated bearer of a useless faith. Earlier in the psalm, he spoke of his feet almost slipping as he envied the success of those who opposed righteousness, while he was waiting for God to show up. Asaph was on the journey, just like me.

However, when he stepped back and considered eternity, the curtains of his depression cracked open, for he saw the end of the game and God's final judgment. When he reminded himself of the larger, eternal picture, he turned from spiritual fatigue to renewed faith. Like Asaph, I get tired and wonder if it's all worth it. Like Asaph, simply seeing the end of the story can be enough encouragement to walk one more mile.

What do you do when you see none of the fruit for which you've been planting seed? What do you do when those you trusted have abandoned you for greener pastures or even thrown you under the bus? What do you do when you feel alone on the journey? One of the best starting points in rebooting your faith is the sanctuary of God, remembering our final destiny. To the church in Galatia, Paul challenged some of the first Christ-followers to *"not become weary in doing good, for at the proper time we will reap a harvest if we do not give up"* (Gal. 6:9). Earlier, Paul reminded the Corinthians to *"stand firm. Let nothing move you. Always give yourselves fully to the work of the Lord, because you know that your labor in the Lord is not in vain"* (1 Cor. 15:58).

Sometimes, the greatest acts of faith are simply trusting God, even when everything and everyone around you is falling apart. Or at least it appears that way. I think of my friend Leo, one of the most encouraging people I know on the planet. He almost always has a smile on his face and has a natural ability to point out the best in others. People love being around him and are better off after being in his company. Leo is excited about life, and his attitude is a breath of fresh air. From the outside, you'd think everything in Leo's life was in order, but he went years on dialysis. Despite the pain and uncertainty, he still reached out to others. The nurses at the dialysis center always said he was their favorite patient. Why? Because Leo saw beyond the present suffering that was plaguing his life.

This whole business is the central question in the book of Job. Is God truly good, or is he a punisher? If you know the account of

Job, you know he was an honest man who loved God and others. He did what was right in the eyes of God and man. But then his life fell apart, and in one day he lost all his children and all his wealth. Later, he also lost his health. His wife told him to just curse God and die. But Job pressed on. He questioned God. He maybe even shook his fist once or twice. But he never called into question his belief in God or God's sovereignty. He kept pressing on, even when his friends told him to throw in the towel.

Sometimes, all it takes to get back in the saddle again is a reminder that although the fight is tough and the road is long, there is victory for those who know Christ and the power of his resurrection. Be encouraged. The race is worth it, the victory is sure, and the reward is greater than you can imagine.

The Forgiveness Factor

Sometimes, to really go forward, we have to cut ties with the past. We have to forgive the past and let it go. That's what forgiveness means, anyway. There are times when people get the wrong idea of what forgiveness is. That's why the concept is so hard and unrealistic at times.

Forgiveness doesn't mean that we go around with a fake smile on our faces, pretending nothing ever happened. Forgiveness also doesn't mean that we jump back into a relationship with an unrepentant person. In the first church, the apostle Paul warned a young evangelist, Timothy, to stay away from a metal worker named Alexander because he had caused harm to the church (2 Tim. 4:14). Paul warned Timothy, but he didn't go on and on about the guy.

In a very real sense, forgiveness is simply letting the other person off the hook. It doesn't mean you feel good, especially at first. It just means you let it go. After all, the whole of the gospel message is that Jesus forgives us. Yup, I had to let Doug and others go.

A few years ago, I was taking some down time in the front range of Colorado. Next to Lake Tahoe, it's one of my most favorite places on the globe. This wasn't family vacation time; it was getting-away-with-God time. I had written out my pains on a sheet of paper, and I planned to literally bury the past. I drove my rental car, a small SUV, up Pikes Peak, the highest mountain in the United States that you can drive all the way to the top. I love it up there. You can see for miles. I feel a sense of power and wonder being on top of the world. I probably spent an hour not talking to anyone, just walking and climbing around the summit. Armed with my camera, I took shots at some of the colorful foliage that only lives at 14,100 feet and only blooms for a couple of months in the summer.

One of my favorite pictures now hangs in my kitchen. The shot has a blue sky in the background dotted with periodic clouds, with a foreground of yellow, blue, purple, and pink flowers in a quilt of green grass. The air was as pure as it can be, and the breeze was just enough to make me glad I brought a light jacket. The beauty of God's creation was revitalizing. Before I headed back, I wandered about a hundred yards down a rough path, away from the parking area and into a small boulder field. There, with no one but me and my creator, I took my page of pains and confessions and dropped them into a hole underneath some stones freshly revealed from the melted ice. I acknowledged the pain. It was real. But I had to move on.

It helps to look at the larger picture. Paul noted in Romans 8:28 that in the midst of pain, God can work things out in ways we can't possibly imagine. At the end of Genesis, Joseph forgave his brothers who sold him into slavery and recognized that God had providentially orchestrated something good despite their evil choices.

Looking back to that ominous day years ago, I don't believe Doug had any evil intent in his heart. While I still believe he made the wrong choice, I believe he did the best he could. Often, we have a tendency to extend grace to ourselves but are a bit cheap in granting it to others. I was finally able to let go of Doug's betrayal. I also believe that God will eventually bring good out of it. He already has.

Finding My Forgiveness

Someone once said that Satan has a way of knowing which of our buttons to push. My past sin is a big red button for me, and the evil one knows it. Sometimes, it comes out of nowhere. I'm doing life, and from some unseen trigger, I remember a sin, a lie, or a moment from the past when I blew it. Sometimes, it comes when I'm doing preacher things and studying the Bible; the evil one turns God's word into a tool of accusation against me. I've already come forward on my sexual experiences in high school and junior college. That was a long time ago, but from time to time, the voice of the enemy reminds me of it. A number of years ago, we were serving a small-town church in Northern Indiana when I found myself on the mat with Satan, wrestling for my life.

I was sitting in my office studying when the sun came through the window, creating a warm and peaceful atmosphere with a northern Indiana winter outside. I was working through a passage on church leadership when I came face-to-face with the question of my worthiness to be a pastor. At least that's how the accusation came. The text was 1 Timothy 3 where the apostle Paul gives a picture of biblical leadership and service. In this snapshot of a godly leader, Paul notes that the elder is the *"husband of one wife"* (1 Tim 3:2 KJV).

The literal Greek translation of this phrase is something along the lines of a one-woman man. But how do you interpret that phrase? Some scholars take it lightly, with the suggestion that Paul admonished a culture of polygamy and therefore only men who were presently married to only one woman were qualified. Others interpret the passage quite literally, and thus anyone who has ever been married more than once for any reason is disqualified.

On the one hand, the commentator was right to elevate marriage since God also honors it. If a man is flippant about marriage, he has no business leading others. But on the other hand, a more legalistic interpretation without context and love misses the point. If we take the passage without the full context of a loving leader, then a guy who treats his wife like a dog could be qualified. Yup, he's only been married once. But no one wants to follow a guy who is cruel to and uncaring of his wife. However, that wasn't my cause for concern. The commentator went on to describe any sexual relationships, anytime, outside of marriage as reason to keep a person out of church leadership. There it was. My past was present in my mind, and according to this religious expert, I was out.

Was I condemned? Was I too broken by my own sin to preach God's word and lead in his church? Then I sensed the spirit of God asking me to take a deep breath and review what I did know.

"Did you sin in this, Steve?"

"Yes, most definitely!"

"Any excuses on this?"

"No. I confess openly and honestly that I did it."

"Do you believe that Jesus died on the cross for those sins?"

"Yes."

"Do you believe that my son, Jesus, rose from the grave and that his payment was enough?"

"Yes."

"Did you accept my grace and what Jesus did on the cross for you? Did you not make a choice to repent of your sins, be baptized, and follow me?"

"Yes."

"So, are your sins not forgiven then?"

"Yes, yes, they are."

"Then let it go!"

As in other times of darkness when my pain or memories of guilt piled high like a thousand pounds weighing on my soul, God stepped in and reminded me of the bigger picture and the hope in him. I just had to let the negative go and hold on. That's really how you make it through sometimes—one step of hope at a time.

CHAPTER 8
SOMETIMES I STILL WONDER

We may be in the dark about what God is doing,
but we are not in the dark about God.

—Os Guinness

God never made a promise that was too good to be true.

—Dwight L. Moody

I'm sure it was a Saturday afternoon. Third grade, I believe. My adopted dad dropped me off at an old theater on south Western Street by myself to see the opening showing of *The Empire Strikes Back*. I don't know why I was alone other than I probably didn't want to wait for a friend and knew my dad had no interest in seeing the universe saved from the Dark Side. That was back in the day when you could see an early afternoon flick for a buck fifty. I had enough for a ticket with a quarter left over to call Dad after Luke Skywalker was victorious and the credits rolled. I stood in the long line and patiently waited my turn to get a ticket and find a seat before the action started.

What I didn't know is that the economics of *Star Wars* and the theater had raised their entrance price to $2, making me a quarter short. I looked at the lady on the other side of the glass, and she looked back. I looked at the dad and his family behind me with an expression that said something along the lines of, "Aren't you a man of compassion? Don't you care for this poor soul of a kid?" But his expression said, "Get along, kid, we're waiting." So before the crowd rioted, I quietly stepped out of line and used my call-home quarter to ask my dad to come and get me. Dad came, offered no solution to my dilemma, and drove me home. That was it. No one cared. Of course, that was all incredibly small compared to big-world problems like starvation, persecution, and oppression. But in that moment, it was a big deal for me.

There are still times that my flesh wonders if God cares. I know he does in my faith and in my head, but my emotions don't always follow. Part of the faith struggle is also a purpose-of-life struggle, or rather how we look at life. Having a wrong understanding of faith can get us in trouble because it affects how we interpret life. The question is not only whether or not God is good but whether life is supposed to be fair and easy.

If our goal is to secure the easy life, then we're going to come up empty all the time. Going back to God and man in Genesis, we find that after sin entered the picture, all of creation was messed up as well. Thorns came on the scene, thwarting Adam's work with the soil (Gen. 3:17–18). Life was no longer easy. And life is no longer easy today, either, but it can be good.

Does God Really Take Care of Our Needs?

Finding the good in life is often connected with our understanding of the difference between what we want and what we truly need. One of the first lessons God gave me in clarifying the difference came when I was about 17. I was expecting a car stereo for Christmas; I got a couple of tires. Earlier that fall, I had acquired my first car, a gray 1979 Pontiac LeMans. One of the youth leaders called it the Silver Bullet. I loved it. But it had a generic AM/FM radio, and I wanted a stereo cassette player. While I didn't want the tires, I needed them.

God hasn't always given me what I wanted, but he's always given me what I needed, when I needed it. I could wax on about God's provision, even in the dark days. One funny story comes from the week that Debi and I came back to the states after a two-month internship in Russia in 1993. We had given our last cash to a missionary, Max Goins, and had jobs lined up for when we got home. The problem was that one does not get paid until after one works. So that first Sunday night home, we looked ahead to a very bleak week with one loaf of bread and two apples in our little duplex on 3rd and Wall Street. And we prayed. The following morning, one of my college friends came by our place and asked if we liked pimento cheese. His father worked at a food packing company, and they had an overabundance of pimento cheese to get rid of. So for a week, we ate pimento cheese sandwiches for breakfast, lunch, and dinner, with two apples somewhere in the mix. It wasn't about whether we liked pimento cheese. It was about God taking care of our needs.

The scriptures are replete with promises and pictures of God's provision. History is chock-full of testimonies from God's children experiencing God's work in miraculous ways. The autobiography of George Müller is one of my favorite examples. In the nineteenth century, Müller started numerous orphanages in England while serving as a preacher. His story is colored time and time again with testimonies of God's provision, even at the last minute.

I had a professor in college who once noted that God is rarely on time but never late. One of my favorite missionaries, Hudson Taylor, once declared that "God's work done in God's way will never lack God's supplies."[1] That faith is demonstrated and illustrated in scripture in numerous places. Here are a few starter verses to remind you of God's promises of provision:

- *"Who provides food for the raven when its young cry out to God and wander about for lack of food?"* (Job 38:41).

- *"The lions may grow weak and hungry, but those who seek the Lord lack no good thing"* (Ps. 34:10).
- *"So do not worry, saying, 'What shall we eat?' or 'What shall we drink?' or 'What shall we wear?' For the pagans run after all these things, and your heavenly Father knows that you need them"* (Matt. 6:31–32).
- *"Consider the ravens: They do not sow or reap, they have no storeroom or barn; yet God feeds them. And how much more valuable you are than birds!"* (Luke 12:24).
- *"And my God will meet all your needs according to the riches of his glory in Christ Jesus"* (Phil. 4:19).

The father of all creation has promised to take care of his children. Keep looking up to the God who never lets his children down. It may require a daily and even moment-by-moment walk of faith as you live out the kingdom of heaven, but God has proved his faithfulness in the past and will continue in the future.

The funny thing about that cassette stereo player I wanted all those years ago is that it is outdated now. But tires are still all the rage and still quite needed.

Further Thoughts on Faith

Again, there's a misunderstanding about faith and God. The idea that if you truly follow him there will be smooth sailing is not reality. We looked at Job, but there were others. There is a catalog of great men and women in Hebrews 11 who didn't get the easy way out.

There were others who were tortured, refusing to be released so that they might gain an even better resurrection. Some faced jeers and flogging, and even chains and imprisonment. They were put to death by stoning; they were sawed in two; they were killed by the sword. They went about in sheepskins and goatskins, destitute, persecuted and mistreated—the world was not worthy of them. They wandered in deserts and mountains, living in caves and in holes in the ground (Heb. 11:35–38).

Faith doesn't mean you're going to have it easy, but it does mean you're holding on to the promises of God, even when life doesn't feel so easy.

That also begs the question of whether or not life is supposed to be easy. If we return to Genesis one more time, we find that God made it very clear that sin and the curse affected the physical world. God told Adam that working the ground would be hard because of weeds and thorns. But even before everything fell, when Adam and Eve walked in peace with each other and God, they were still called to work the land. There was no curse, but work was still part of their lives. The idea of achieving a life without work is truly not biblical. Sometimes, our problem is that we are doing the wrong work, things we aren't good at or passionate about. But we are still created to work. Sin and brokenness just make work much more difficult. If our life's goal is leisure and perfection, we will always be frustrated.

Sometimes, there are seasons of tremendous success, and James makes it clear that every good and perfect thing is from God. Some people are more gifted and talented than the rest of us, and success seems to come much more easily. Often, though, faith is really demonstrated through tough times.

Returning to Job, we see that Satan claimed that the only reason Job worshiped God was that God was blessing him. But God knew Job's heart and allowed Satan to bring destruction into his life. Still, Job's faith stood strong, and while Job didn't get everything right, he always worshiped God. At the end of it all, the latter part of Job's life was blessed more than the former.

I've had to remind myself of that at times. When I've pressed hard and seen so few results, I've had to remind myself of the bigger picture. While I do not see everything, I can still trust God who does see the end of the story, and it truly is a good end.

CHAPTER 9

I HATE BEING A NICE PASTOR

If you want everyone to like you,
don't be a pastor, go sell ice-cream.

—Dr. Ed Stetzer

The office of preaching is an arduous task. I have often said that
if I could come down with a good conscience, I would rather be
stretched upon a wheel and carry stones than preach one sermon.
But we're stuck with it now. If I had known, I would not have
let myself be drawn into it with twenty-four horses.

—Martin Luther

The most important thing a pastor does is stand in a pulpit every
Sunday and say, 'Let us worship God.' If that ceases to be the
primary thing I do in terms of my energy, my imagination, and
the way I structure my life, then I no longer function as a pastor.

—Eugene H. Peterson

The problem with the word *pastor* in the English language is
that it means almost everything, so it sometimes doesn't mean anything—anything specific, that is. The problem with me is that I tried

to do and to be everything associated with the word, and it nearly killed me.

Think of all the ways this word is used and in all the ways it's applied. What comes to mind when you think of a pastor? He's the older guy everyone loves and who's always there for weddings, funerals, birthdays, and child dedications. He is wise, kind, and always available with practical advice. He's an expert in deciphering the Bible and maybe even reads it in the original Greek and Hebrew. The pastor is the guy who is nice to talk to about whatever is bugging you while he drives you to the airport so you don't have to call Uber.

Of course, he's also the guy who preaches on Sunday mornings. Then there are really famous pastors who do nothing but preach on radio and television programs. If you call a Christian radio station such as Air 1, you can talk to a pastor about whatever is causing you grief or confusion. I took my girls to a Christian rock concert the other day, and between bands, a guy got up to speak for a few minutes, introducing himself as a pastor traveling with the tour. Wow! Cool! What does that mean, and how can I apply for that job? Another pastor does nothing but travel and preach in third-world areas on the map. A friend of mine who has no formal theological training leads an amazing parachurch ministry and is sometimes called a pastor. The list goes on and on.

The problem is that very few, if any, actually carry out all the assumed roles of a pastor at the same time, or at least not very well if they tried. The people who wear the title *pastor* and preach on nationally syndicated radio programs hardly ever make hospital calls. Those who are great at pastoral organizational management and leadership sometimes don't preach any better sermons than a young guy right out of Bible college. Should pastors be skilled and responsible for everything? Is there more to the story, and do we simply not have the right understanding of what an elusive pastor is actually called to?

I sensed God tugging at my heart very soon after I gave my life to Jesus Christ. While I can't remember the exact text, I remember being at a big church with my uncle, listening to the preacher's sermon and experiencing this overwhelming sense that I would be doing the same thing someday. It was the actual proclamation of the message of Christ that drew me to full-time Christian ministry. Maybe that's why I see myself more as a *preacher* than a *pastor*. But it's not like that for every pastor. I know some great guys who don't really like preaching and would rather spend all their days in one-on-one discipleship. But in short, when I answered God's call in this area, I had no idea that full-time Christian ministry would be defined by so many different job descriptions by so many different people.

Bible college was a great experience for me—not to mention it was the place where I married the hottest babe on the planet. I knew I was there with a purpose. I wanted to preach God's word and lead others to a real relationship with him. I had the vision, hunger, and passion for evangelism and the forward progress of the church. Those things still invigorate me today. I think the disconnect and drain eventually came from all the other expectations that tag along with the title *pastor*, the expectations of the people and myself.

After Debi and I came back from the mission field and settled into a local church in northern Indiana, I enjoyed pretty much all of it—the small talk, the weddings, the funerals, the hospital calls, and everything that went along with being a nice small-town pastor. I was doing a good job at it, and our church family was growing. I was salt and light in the local community. After we'd been there a few years, nearly everyone knew me, and I had met almost everyone at least once. It was a good ministry, and we baptized nearly 50 people in a town of 500. My friend Laura, who is still the town clerk, dubbed me the village priest, and that pretty much described what I did and, in some eyes, who I was. I had become a nice pastor.

There are perks, I suppose, of being the village priest, like when you're rushing to the hospital and you have reserved pastor parking places available. Those reserved slots were handy when the guy with the red Suzuki motorcycle took up an entire parking spot in regular parking for his one bike. Is it legal for a pastor to pick up someone's bike and move it onto the grass? Or throw it into the lake? Assuming not, I still thought about it. In addition, many hospitals will give clergy discounts in the cafeteria, a nice treat when you're living on a small salary.

I don't like being called Pastor Steve, but I've pulled the pastor card a few times. There was a guy who really needed to go on a men's retreat, but he didn't want to. He was one of those guys who kept calling me pastor, so I called him out on it. "If I'm your pastor," I said, "then do what I say and go to this event." Okay, maybe I was a bit more diplomatic than that. You can pull rank in the military, so I figured I'd do the same. He was a retired Army master sergeant, after all. I'm happy to report that it worked, and my retired sergeant friend went to the men's event and was extremely blessed.

Part of the problem is an unclear and predominant cultural expectation of who this mysterious pastor is and what that pastor is supposed to do. The apostle Paul wrote about leadership in the church.

> Christ himself gave the apostles, the prophets, the evangelists, the pastors and teachers, to equip his people for works of service, so that the body of Christ may be built up until we all reach unity in the faith and in the knowledge of the Son of God and become mature, attaining to the whole measure of the fullness of Christ (Eph. 4:11–13).

Two things immediately jump out at me in those verses. The first is that there is more than one person doing multiple things that today are all thrust upon the pastor. The other is in the defined goal of the pastor: to *equip* the people to serve God. That is what the Bible calls for in church leadership. The problem is that we often expect the official pastor to do the serving while everyone else sits around and receives the services of the experts. People become consumers of the pastor's professional services. They pay their dentist to fill cavities, their mechanic to change the oil, and their pastor to do the religious stuff. Sure, there is a special skillset connected to the call of a pastor, just like a mechanic or dentist. But we don't expect the dentist to actually brush our teeth every day or the mechanic to fill our car with gas. Somehow, people expect pastors to do the things they should be doing themselves.

One of the problems with this thinking is the belief that pastors are somehow more holy than the rest simply because of their job title. That's one reason I don't like being called Pastor Steve. I'm no more holy than the next guy, regardless of my profession or title. Sure, I'll pray for people. But that doesn't make my prayer any better than the prayer of an accountant who walks with Jesus.

This mentality also takes the responsibility and joy off the rest of the body of believers. It's really easy to assign the religious life to the professional while others sit around and gripe about what they don't like. It's again the secular-versus-the-sacred myth—the idea that a pastor does religious stuff, and an engineer does secular stuff. So we'll let pastors do their jobs and engineers do theirs. The reality is that everything we do is sacred.

My angst hit a critical point one day when some friends gave me a compliment, and because of my brokenness, I couldn't accept it. I was visiting a new couple who were considering joining our church family. As I sat in their immaculate living room looking out the back windows across their yard onto a picturesque golf green and lake, the woman thanked me for my time. She then commented that I was such a nice pastor. I felt like I was going to explode.

Nice? I was fed up and sick of being a nice pastor. Nice is great and all, but so what? When the world needs saving, people don't call for a nice guy. Tony Stark, Rambo, and Batman aren't necessarily known for being nice, but they get the job done. People are saved and the world is made free from the evil that lurks in the shadows by guys who are focused and tough and powerful.

The problem was not with the couple but with me. When she said *nice*, I saw years of word images like *safe, routine, boring*, and *status quo* flash through my heart. That tension came from the unclear expectation of what my calling was and is. I was doing the job of a nice village priest, yet the original calling in my heart was evangelism and kingdom advancement more than being social. There is a place for pastoral concern and niceness, but that was not my first calling. Niceness was the bulk of what I was doing, and I was dying inside.

It was more than the assumed role, though; it was a depletion deep within my own being. After years of casual conversations, my ability to engage in small talk had come to a close. While I'm quite an adventurous guy, there are times when I'm held captive by a twinge of introversion. To some extent, it's probably not just me. Over the years, I've seen numerous studies noting that women speak 10,000–20,000 more words in a normal day than many men. That is certainly the case with Debi and me. I once read that President Reagan, the Great Communicator, was actually pretty bad at small talk. That encouraged me because sometimes I feel like President 40 and I are cut from the same cloth. There are times when I'm burned out from talking, socializing, and trying to fix other people's problems. Once I knew I was broken inside, I didn't know how to fix it. So I kept my mask on and kept going forward.

There is also a broad misunderstanding that Jesus was nice. Sure, he was nice to the children, widows, and downtrodden. But he was also bold and brash toward those who abused the message of God. He didn't waste time responding to fake seekers such as Herod or pandering to the religious establishment when it hindered people from finding God. Jesus didn't care what anyone thought or what their expectations were because he was clear about who he was and what his mission was.

That was part of my problem. I had a mission and a purpose. Then I started to doubt myself tremendously, doubt that probably was rooted in my unstable youth.

Managing Expectations

I was sitting at my computer desk on a Sunday afternoon during Hurricane Harvey. All kinds of options went through my head. Who should I be checking up on? A grandmother in the community had passed away that morning, so I braved potential flood waters to go over and visit, pray, and comfort the family. Then, since I'd ventured out, I checked on the church building. What else? Part of me wanted to avail myself to the nearest fire department, but I'm not qualified to be a fireman, a volunteer fireman, or even the son of a fireman. But I am an Eagle Scout, and many times people just need help with physical labor. I could do that. Then, I remembered that with the lack of current demands on my time, I could work on this book, and maybe the best use of my time was to get this monster finished while I had a chance.

That mental and emotional debate on the day of a hurricane is probably quite similar to many days in my life. There are tons of options, and the bottom line is that no matter which route I take, someone is going to be disappointed. That is especially true of pastors in a small local church. If I spend all my time trying to reach people who don't know Jesus, then I'm neglecting some shepherding or pastoral duties. If I spend all my time trying to be an entrepreneurial leader, it shows with a shallow sermon on Sunday. I have a friend in ministry who is the biggest people-person-pastor I know. But there are times when he borrows sermons from someone else to preach on Sunday. I'm not slamming the guy for that, just noting that it's almost impossible to do it all. The list goes on and on, and sometimes, I wish I could check out and just change tires, or maybe run for president.

Sometimes, I Wish I Was a Marine

My friend Bobby and I spent a number of hours at the Marine recruiting station the summer between eighth and ninth grade. Years later, the week before I headed to Bible college, I got a call from one of the recruiters who found my name someplace in the records. I'm not sure why I never pursued the Marine Corps or any other military option as a career. Even my friend Brad and I wondered seriously one year what it would take to make it into West Point. But considering all branches of the military, it's the Marines that really count. Don't tell my Army brother-in-law or my Air Force sister-in-law who served as a nurse that I said so, or they'll never ask me to pray at a Thompson family reunion again. On the other hand, that might not be a bad thing. Why does the pastor always get to pray?

But the Marines are tough. They get things done, and America owes a lot of respect to those men and women who have served valiantly in harm's way. That is probably why my second son joined the Marine Corps. My boy is smart and strong, and he wanted to serve before he launched into whatever career God would take him. The Marines were the right choice for him. And you've got to admit that the Marines really do have the coolest recruitment commercials.

Yes, there are times when I wish I was in the Marines or the Army, a general leading battalions into action. I've even used an illustration about my wife and shopping. Deb takes some time when it comes to shopping. Even though she has a list, there are always other things that catch her eye and because of some value or another wind up in her shopping cart. I like to say that I shop like a Marine or a Navy Seal. I get in, get what I need, and get out. A big part of it is feeling like the mission is clear and the outcome is clearly measurable. When is it done, and how did we do? Measuring ministry isn't always done in concrete ways.

At times, it's hard to see if you've done anything good in the ministry, at least beyond the hype. If a preacher gets thousands of people into a church building on a Sunday, people assume he's a success. Maybe he is. But that's not always the case. Don't get me wrong; I believe all churches are to grow and expand. But considering the bigger picture, numbers don't always mean long-term success. The real success comes when hearts are changed and they go out to change other hearts. Real change happens when people connect others to Jesus without the official pastor having anything to do with it. In Acts 11:19, unknown individuals, not pastors, stepped out of their comfort zones to share Jesus with people who were different from them, and the amazing Antioch church was formed.

It's easy to see the flash; it's hard to see those quiet moments when Christians are loving on their neighbors. You don't always know it's even happened. It's quite possible that some of the best preachers in our time are the ones who've hidden themselves to faithfully preach to small churches and make a difference in the lives of a few people. These people are the ones who go out and change the world. But you don't always see them, those quiet preachers who set off the whole revival. A Marine, on the other hand, is tough and focused and produces measurable results. When Marines produce, they know it and are told so by their commanding officer. "Good job, Marine!"

I turned 49 this year, so I'm too old be a Marine. I am more focused, though, and I'm reminded often what Christ has promised to say at the end of all things: *Well done, good and faithful servant!* (Matt. 25:21).

Going back to Ephesians 4, part of the answer lies with the certainty that all who wear the name of Christ are to intentionally love the world around them. The pastor and other leaders are to help the saints do their jobs. Not only does every person have a purpose, but that purpose is included in the greater kingdom of God in which every Christian participates. This principle is what theologians call the priesthood of believers. In 1 Peter 2:9, the apostle notes that we are all a *"chosen people, a royal priesthood, a holy nation, God's special possession, that you may declare the praises of him who called you out of darkness into his wonderful light."*

Did you get that? Peter clearly states that everyone who wears the name of Jesus is part of his priesthood. Yes, there are people called to full-time ministry, just like others are called and created for other places in life such as medicine or education. But there are many parts of daily ministry that do not require a theology degree and are uniquely situated for lots of people to do. In any healthy church body, there are numerous people and leaders who can and should do what's often placed on the preacher's desk.

As I've already said, when I go to my wife's extended family reunion, I'm often asked to pray before the meal. And again, why me? I'm not the Thompson patriarch. But I wear the name *pastor*, so it's just assumed I'm the guy for the job. Maybe you can tell them what I said about the Marine Corps.

At one of the lowest points in my ministry, I got a call from a member of our church informing me that his wife was in the hospital. Within seconds of talking with my friend, I was overcome with despondence. I thought, "If someone else calls me wanting something, I'm going to kill myself." It wasn't that I disliked these people; I just didn't have any emotional energy left. If you take a dishrag and squeeze it and twist it, eventually there will be nothing in it to wring out. Dry. It's just dry.

People want to know that someone cares for them, and I get that. I want that. But when everyone looks to the pastor to do all the caring, there just isn't enough to go around, at least not for long. Whether people realize it or not, they just want someone, anyone, to care. It doesn't have to be the pastor.

As a teenager, I never had a close relationship with the youth minister in my home church. There was no problem; it was just a big church. But there were people in my church who did care for me. That's what we need. Bob was one of those men who took time to engage me, and I still talk to him on the phone once in a while all these years later. That's what everyone needs—not so much an official pastor but someone who cares. Bob doesn't call me pastor, although many times he does call me rabbi, which is okay because I know he's joking, and, well, I'm not Jewish.

Recently, Debi told me that it's probably okay to be a nice pastor. "After all," she said, "there are a whole lot of people out there who aren't nice." I knew she was right. I see it all the time, and I know enough people in the marketplace to know it's true. There are some really selfish and jerky people out there.

When the people of the world meet others like me who are different from the usual cutthroats, they see the difference, and the difference could possibly draw them closer to knowing God. My desire is that everyone who wears the name of Jesus would be, well, nice. But I suppose I should start by leading the way. Maybe I can pull the pastor card on them and just tell them to be nice. Be nice, everyone!

When the church grasps this, we'll see a lot more people truly being the hands and feet of Jesus. When more people in the church realize these truths, more people will be encouraged and blessed by Christ. That is a good thing. So maybe being called a nice pastor isn't such a bad thing after all.

CHAPTER 10
THE VISION OF OTHERS

Two roads diverged in a yellow wood.

—Robert Frost

You must put your head into the lion's mouth
if the performance is to be a success.

—Winston Churchill

I'm not afraid of failure; I'm afraid of succeeding
at things that don't matter.

—William Carey

The summer following seventh grade was about the time the little kid in me started to die. Now to be clear, we are made to grow up, mature, and take responsibility. That's not what I'm talking about. For me, it was seeing the goofy seventh-grade class picture of me in the Sam Houston Jr. High yearbook and not liking myself. My hair was all messed up, my shirt was wrinkled, and my teeth were still very crooked, even with braces. I started changing to compensate, so by the eighth grade, my picture bore no smile but rather the serious look of Mr. Spock on *Star Trek*—or really, the serious look of my uncle. It's not that I didn't do anything childish that summer or after. In fact, the summer after seventh grade was when some of my friends and I got buzzes. We looked like little Marines, and I felt like one, too. But the real thrill came when the ninth-grade girls rubbed their hands on my head when they passed me in the halls.

No, it wasn't as much a change in action as it was a change in heart. It was a wrong vision of who I thought I needed to be. I looked up to my uncle, who was probably the main male role model in my life, and for a while I thought he was perfect. Looking at myself in that seventh-grade picture, I knew I was light-years from perfection, and no one was telling me anything different. So I decided to change and become like my uncle, who was all about being serious.

My uncle is great. He's brilliant and the one who led me to Jesus. He's smart, confident, and competent in almost everything he does. But, kind of like the accountants, he was way behind me in the adventure quotient. As an adult, I can be quite serious at times and think very deeply. Even as a kid I thought about big issues and watched the world news. The difference is that while my uncle knew everything about everything in those big issues of news and life, I wanted to go out and actually do something—to change the world. I wanted to jump on a plane and go to those places and do something about the wrongs in the world. But at the time, I didn't have enough self-assurance to declare who I was and why in the world God put me on this planet.

I see this drama played out all the time in the world. It's quite sad. I talk with women who keep dating losers because they don't feel as if they are worth anyone better. Sometimes, it's a family expectation. My friend Tom had to work through a relationship with his father after he announced he wasn't going to take over the family business but instead go into ministry. Tom pursued what he believed God called him to do and now leads academics at a major US seminary. If he had followed the course set for him by his father, he may have been making more money, but he and the world would have missed out on a bigger, eternal blessing.

In our church plant in Northern California, there was a little bit of that surrogate vision as well. The project was more the church planting organization's vision than mine. My original vision was to plant a church in another major city in the United States where I'd anticipated being for the rest of my life. None of those pieces were moving yet, and these folks kept talking to me about starting a church in California and told me all the reasons I should look into it. When I laid out what was on my heart to one of the movers and shakers in the church planting movement, he listened for a while and then changed the direction of our conversation like one of those county roads in the mountains of Colorado. You think you're heading straight, and suddenly you're facing the opposite horizon.

That same conversation played out a number of times for a year or so, and I eventually said yes, not really wanting to. They had a powerful vision of multiple churches springing up all over California. It was a great vision, and in a general sense, it was near to my heart to get people and Jesus connected. But it wasn't what my heart had been longing for. The problem was not that I wasn't called and equipped to start a new evangelistic church; it was just the wrong time, place, and vision. It was someone else's vision.

Now here's the tension. More and more in our culture, self-actualization is being elevated above responsibility. That's especially dangerous for those who are pursuing Jesus, as he himself noted that he came to serve and not to be served. There are times in our self-centered culture when adults need to put selfish and childish actions and attitudes away. Part of the growth process is merely realizing that mature men and women need to take a deep breath and do what's right, regardless of how they feel.

I like the illustration from the movie *Glory Road*, where coach Don Haskins gives a reality check to one of the best players who's not living up to his full potential. Haskins sees his player, Bobby Hill, throwing his gift away and recounts the life of his father who worked hard to provide for his family and give them the chance at a life he never had. He put his family first.

After catching Bobby breaking curfew with a girl, Haskins takes him to the stadium to run up and down the steps. After an outburst by Hill, there's a pause, and the coach tells the young athlete that his "old man drove a truck for the better part of his life. Now there ain't nothing wrong with that, other than the fact that he hated it. But, Hill, that's the only way he knew how to put food on the table and give his kids a chance to do something they loved."[1]

Again, if our sole goal in life is ease and feeling happy, we're going to be disappointed. While we can find joy and adventure in life, we still have to work, and work hard. The problem is allowing others—not God—to define us or our life's ministry.

Owning Failure and Releasing Theirs

When I look back at our time in California and the church we started, I see the mistakes I made in the process. I made some poor strategic decisions. It's good to admit our mistakes so we can learn from them and because it is the right thing to do. We need to own our decisions in a culture consumed with a victim mentality.

Even with the mixed vision of everyone involved with the church in California, I own the fact that ultimately it came down to me. While the others may not have honored my vision, I'm still responsible for my actions. I should have stood my ground and insisted that this was not the right call at the time. It was a good vision, but many times, taking what is good can keep us from taking the best.

Growing in maturity requires us to own our faults and failures. It also means that part of a healthy life requires building appropriate boundaries and refusing to take credit for negative things done to us or around us. The worst illustration of this is children of abuse.

They are not at fault for the pain that someone stronger inflicted on them, yet they often feel so. There can be times when the emotional brokenness inside of them still tells them they must have somehow deserved it. Intellectually, they know that is a lie, but the heart doesn't always catch up with the head very easily.

There are many circumstances beyond our control, things that just happen—weather, economics, politics, world affairs. Maybe it's the new neighbors who moved into the house behind you and throw parties until 3:00 in the morning on Saturday nights. Every time that happens, aren't we always tempted to show up and ring their doorbell at 5:00 a.m. when we get up? I want to, but I don't. At least I haven't yet. But good leaders are able to roll with the punches and navigate through them. It's a bit trickier for those still wrestling with their own stories. I've spent time in that neighborhood, too.

While I have owned my mistakes, there are and were factors outside my control. The growth projections for the region where we planted the church in 2004 were off the charts. The movement began, and then the housing market and all the markets shut down a few years later. People lost their homes and moved away. New houses weren't being built, and families didn't move in. The target area for our new church community dwindled quickly. At the outset of the project, I was assigned a strategic mentor. The problem was that he had never planted a church from scratch as we were doing. He was a great guy, but his suggestions and tips weren't exactly what we needed.

Two years into the project, we had a meeting, and he asked me for more details on how I was raising money for the work. He never had to raise funds for the church he planted because he'd launched with a core group of about 100 people from another church. The dynamics of the initial phases of our projects were totally different. I left so many of those meetings frustrated because so little of it applied to us. But the church planting group wanted me to meet with the mentor, and I did because that was the responsible thing to do.

The church planting group made promises that didn't come to fruition, and, on a funny note, I didn't even like the name of the church. My vision was to settle there for a while and let the name of this new creation kind of simmer and evolve. But because of the logistical direction and data the church planting group was running with, they wanted a name on the project even before we arrived in California. So, to comply with their vision, I came up with one in an afternoon, and we ran with it.

I'm not saying all this to slam anyone, and I do own my mistakes. This is simply to show that it's so easy to fall in line with what someone else wants when we're not grounded in who we are in Christ and comfortable with that, no matter what anyone else says or does. Sure, there are seasons when we do what we have to do because we have a goal in mind, but when it turns into a pattern of pleasing, we wind up with mountains of heartache.

There are times when we just have to say no. It may mean losing a promotion or missing an immediate opportunity. It may mean waiting longer. But the end result will be so much better. One of my doctor friends recently started his own practice, and he noted with a smile that while he is a lot poorer on his own, he is also a lot happier. He could have stayed where he was, following the lead of an established practice that was paying him a whole lot more. But that was not his vision.

Maybe one reason I was slow to make the move to California was that intuitively, I had sensed some dots were not connecting. To illustrate, Jesus sent the apostles out in groups of two. Paul and Barnabas went out on their first missionary journey together, but their vision was to prepare other guys for solo projects, guys who began alone with promised logistical infrastructure from the organization. Many of the best church plants were, indeed, done by solo pastors and their wives. The key, though, is that deep within their souls, the pastors sensed an unwavering call from God to do exactly what they were doing at exactly that time and place.

My general vision of getting people and Jesus connected was in line with the general vision of this church planting group. For that reason, we pressed on for a long time, beyond when other church plants had thrown in the towel. But there were several disconnects in which I didn't feel I could assert myself. I couldn't do some things the way I believed they should be done. I want to state again that I'm not throwing this church planting group under the bus. They have advanced the kingdom and connected thousands of people to Jesus. The problem was that we had two different visions.

Much of my healing and new purpose began as I got closer to truly listening to and hearing God, allowing myself to take on his definition of what it means for Steve Hinton to be a pastor. That was not and is not how the world would always define me. But that's okay. The world, and even Satan, will spend endless energy trying to form us and fit us into what they want. They will tell us what they want us to hear, all in the pursuit of what they believe our mission is. The question now is who we're going to listen to.

CHAPTER 11
WHO SAID THAT?

Falsehoods not only disagree with truths,
but usually quarrel among themselves.

—Daniel Webster

And they say that she's a fallen angel.
I wonder if she recalls when she last flew.

—Rich Mullins

Define yourself radically as one beloved by God.
This is the true self. Every other identity is illusion.

—Brennan Manning

I'm not sure when or why we started calling him Sir Rob. I mean, he's not British, and as far as I know, Queen Elizabeth has not knighted him. But Sir Rob just kind of feels like a knight. He's ex-military and a tough guy, but he carries an air of nobility and wisdom that makes me feel like I'm talking with someone in the British Parliament, except he doesn't have a British accent.

I also don't recall when I first heard him pose this question: "Really? Who said that?" I've heard it a lot, though. Someone begins the degradation process—you know, the I'm-an-idiot talk—and Sir Rob asks, "Really? Who said that?"

I self-deprecated a lot when I first landed in the northwest Houston area. The move was more of a necessity for employment than a sense of calling. The work went well, and the church turned around and thrived again. Despite this new move in the right direction, the voice I was listening to most often was one of despair. In short, the voice kept telling me I was here instead of where I wanted to be because of at least one, if not all three, of the following:

1. I'm a failure.
2. I'm stupid.
3. God just doesn't like me.

But, in the voice of Sir Rob, "Really? Who said that?" In other words, who said I was a failure or stupid or that God doesn't like me?

Sure, we've all failed at things and made mistakes. But that is not the same as *being* a failure. Sometimes we *do* something stupid, but that does not mean we *are* stupid. I believe Sir Rob is on to something. He's asking where the thought came from and what the ramifications are. From a spiritual standpoint, we know that Satan is the father of lies (John 8:44). Jesus said that Satan is on a mission to steal and kill and destroy. One of the ways Satan attacks humanity is in the heart.

It's hard to live to our fullest when we believe the worst about ourselves, and that's what Satan wants. Yes, we have all sinned and fallen short of the glory of God, but that's why Jesus came. The mission of Christ was not only to seek and to save, but to restore. That's why Christians are new creations (2 Cor. 5:17). That is an identity Satan certainly doesn't want us to carry around.

Satan speaks destruction to us through many means. Sometimes, it is the voice of one of our parents, a school teacher, or even a religious nut in our church. Many times, it's through our own broken hearts. For me, it was a combination of them all. That's what was going on that dark night when I thought about ending it all. I was believing the lie of Satan that I was a total failure and of use to no one. But that is not what Jesus says.

Jesus came that we might have life and life to the fullest (John 10:10). This full life begins now when we accept Christ and continues until his second coming at the end of all things. Jesus does not call us failures. Quite the opposite. A quick survey of scripture reveals a more powerful picture of who we are in Jesus. Here are a few illustrations.[1]

- I am more than a conqueror through Christ who loves me (Rom. 8:37).
- I am assured that all things work together for good to those who love him (Rom. 8:28).
- I am a temple, a dwelling place of God. His Spirit and his life dwell in me (1 Cor. 3:16, 6:19).
- I am a new creation (2 Cor. 5:17).
- I am an ambassador for Christ (2 Cor. 5:20).
- I am God's coworker (2 Cor. 6:1).
- I am a minister of reconciliation (2 Cor. 5:17–20).
- I am God's handiwork (Eph. 2:10).
- I am forgiven (Eph. 1:7–8; Col. 1:14).
- I am confident that God will perfect the work he has begun in me (Phil. 1:6).
- I am a citizen of heaven (Phil. 3:20).
- I have been given a spirit of power, love, and self-control instead of fear (2 Tim. 1:7).
- I am a member of a chosen race, a royal priesthood, a holy nation, a people for God's own possession (1 Pet. 2:9–10).

Sometimes, we have to reprogram our thinking with the truth of God to replace the lies of the world. In Psalm 139, David acknowledged that God created his inmost being and therefore gave his life divine purpose. The same applies to us today.

I recently shared Sir Rob's question with a younger friend, and then I followed up with this: "Who are you going to believe?"

Letter from Abba

A while back, Debi and I spent some time with a wise man named John who loves encouraging people in full-time Christian service. In fact, he even created a ministry for pastors called The Blessing Ranch. He's somewhat of a cowboy at heart and lived in the Houston area a few decades ago. He always loved the Houston rodeo, which pretty much consumes the entire month of March. I'm not sure, but the Houston rodeo may be the largest rodeo in the world.

But John is also a highly educated man. Really, his title is Dr. John Walker, and I've already forgotten how many degrees were on his office wall. So Debi and I settled into our seat across from Dr. Walker, burned out like two charred trees after a California forest fire. We were ready to drink in some sorely needed wisdom from this sage.

Eventually, John addressed our thinking and internal programming and challenged me to think something through and then act on it for a few months. In short, the challenge was to create a list of two things: my major life events and turning points with the good, the bad, and the ugly; and a list of scriptures that might speak to those life events or themes. Then, he wanted me to weave those two lists together, to craft them into a letter as though God were writing directly to me. A letter from Abba, he called it. He said to go over that letter at least once a day for at the next eight weeks. As we were wrapping up, this wise but tough cowboy went over to his desk and pulled out his own letter from Abba. The current edition of my letter from Abba has been revised a bit, but I'll share the original draft with you.

Steve,

I see you. I acknowledge you, and I smile when I think about you (Num. 6:24–25). In fact, I made you (Ps. 139:13–15), and I take great delight in you (Zeph. 3:17). I share your adventurous and passionate heart. I'm the one who made this whole shooting match in the first place (Gen. 1–2). I am thrilled that you honor me for that (Rom. 1:20–21). I know your wounds. As I was there when Job was smitten (Job 1–2), I was there with you (Ps. 139:7). I know your feelings of rejection, loneliness, failure, stupidity, and above all else, inadequacy. But those are feelings and not reality.

Yes, many a man has rejected you, but I will vindicate you (Ps. 35:24, 54:1, 135:14). You have sinned and blown it, but I have cleansed you with hyssop and washed you whiter than snow (Ps. 51:7). I know that your current situation is something that the father of lies (John 8:44) has used against you by reinforcing those feelings, but that is not me. My word is good (1 Sam. 15:29). I do not change like the shifting shadows and am thus always there for you (James 1:17). Indeed, I even esteem you (Isa. 66:2).

I have chosen you. You are chosen, a royal priest, holy, my special possession (1 Pet. 2:9) in order that you might declare my praises (1 Pet. 2:9), which you do quite well. You are like the warrior poets from *Braveheart*, and thus, in my presence and the presence of Christ Jesus, I charge you to preach my word in season and out (2 Tim. 4:1–8). You have a heart for the nations as I do (Ps. 2:8). Like my heart, you desire that all men come to know me (1 Tim. 2:4). Steve, at your core, you are powerful (2 Tim. 1:7).

I know that at this time you are tired and beaten down. Like the men of King David who were humiliated by Hanun, King of Amon, you feel dejected (2 Sam. 10:4–5). So come away to me and abide in me (Matt. 11:28, John 15:1–5). Instead of looking to men, *trust* in me with all your heart (Prov. 3:5–6). Keep looking to the big picture. Fix your eyes not on what is seen but on what is unseen (2 Cor. 4:18). Set your heart and mind on things above (Col. 3:1–2).

Yes, it will be a difficult and thorn-infested life (Gen. 3:17–19), but remember that you are in the company of the saints in Hebrews 11. You are walking the path of Abraham, Isaac, and Jacob, who, though they did not receive the complete fulfillment on this side of eternity (Heb. 11:38–40), pressed on anyway in faith (Heb. 11:1, 6).

So press on, too, Steve. Think about that which is true, noble, right, pure, lovely, and admirable, and everything that is excellent or praiseworthy (Phil. 4:8). Guard your heart with ferocity (Prov. 4:23). Be my ambassador (2 Cor. 5:20), and you will eventually see my goodness in the land of the living (Ps. 27:13).

Steve, I am proud of you, son. Keep going; keep going (Matt. 25:21, 23).

—Abba

Selected Scripture References

Numbers 6:24–25: *"The Lord bless you and keep you; the LORD make his face shine on you."*

Psalm 139:13–14: *"For you created my inmost being. . . . I praise you because I am fearfully and wonderfully made."*

Zephaniah 3:17: *"The LORD your God is with you, the Mighty Warrior who saves. He will take great delight in you; in his love he will no longer rebuke you, but will rejoice over you with singing."*

Romans 1:20–21: *"For since the creation of the world God's invisible qualities . . . have been clearly seen. . . . For although they knew God, they neither glorified him as God nor gave thanks to him."*

Psalm 139:7: *"Where can I go from your Spirit? Where can I flee from your presence?"*

Psalm 35:24: *"Vindicate me in your righteousness, LORD my God; do not let them gloat over me."*

Psalm 54:1: *"Save me, O God, by your name; vindicate me by your might."*

Psalm 135:14: *"For the LORD will vindicate his people and have compassion on his servants."*

Psalm 51:7: *"Cleanse me with hyssop, and I will be clean; wash me, and I will be whiter than snow."*

John 8:44: *"When he [the devil] lies, he speaks his native language, for he is a liar and the father of lies."*

1 Samuel 15:29: *"He who is the Glory of Israel does not lie."*

James 1:17: *"Every good and perfect gift is from above, coming down from the Father of the heavenly lights, who does not change like shifting shadows."*

Isaiah 66:2: *"These are the ones I look on with favor: those who are humble and contrite in spirit, and who tremble at my word."*

1 Peter 2:9: *"But you are a chosen people, a royal priesthood, a holy nation, God's special possession, that you may declare the praises of him who called you out of darkness into his wonderful light."*

Psalm 2:8: *"Ask me, and I will make the nations your inheritance, the ends of the earth your possession."*

1 Timothy 2:4: *"Who wants all people to be saved and to come to a knowledge of the truth."*

2 Timothy 1:7: *"For the Spirit God gave us does not make us timid but gives us power, love and self-discipline."*

Matthew 11:28: *"Come to me, all you who are weary and burdened, and I will give you rest."*

Proverbs 3:5–6: *"Trust in the LORD with all your heart and lean not on your own understanding; in all your ways submit to him, and he will make your paths straight."*

2 Corinthians 4:18: *"So we fix our eyes not on what is seen, but on what is unseen, since what is seen is temporary, but what is unseen is eternal."*

Colossians 3:1–2: *"Since, then, you have been raised with Christ, set your hearts on things above, where Christ is, seated at the right hand of God. Set your minds on things above, not on earthly things."*

Hebrews 11:1–2: *"Now faith is confidence in what we hope for and assurance about what we do not see. This is what the ancients were commended for."*

Proverbs 4:23: *"Above all else, guard your heart, for everything you do flows from it."*

2 Corinthians 5:20: *"We are therefore Christ's ambassadors, as though God were making his appeal through us."*

Psalm 27:13: *"I remain confident of this: I will see the goodness of the LORD in the land of the living."*

Matthew 25:21, 23: *"His master replied, 'Well done, good and faithful servant! You have been faithful with a few things; I will put you in charge of many things. Come and share your master's happiness!'"*

Help from *The Help*

At this stage in my life, my two sons have grown and left the house, but my two younger daughters are still at home. One is a senior and the other a junior in high school. All that is to say that our Friday night family times usually center on movies such as *Sabrina* rather than *The Expendables*. A while back, my oldest daughter rented a movie called *The Help*, and while I wasn't excited about the movie, I wanted to be with my girls. So I prepared for a night of Hinton tacos and a girly show. *The Help* is a great movie based on a 2009 novel of the same name. The drama chronicles the stories of African-American maids in Jackson, Mississippi, as recorded by a young white woman during the Civil Rights movement of the early 1960s. Two or three times in the movie, a motherly black maid tells the young white girl that she nannies, "You is kind, you is smart, and you is important."[2] Wow! There is power in that. As the flick finished, I kept coming back to that scene and its power. We don't know how it all turned out, but the assumption was that a child growing up with regular positive reinforcement is much more likely to succeed than one who is ignored or condemned. That practice is so crucial.

The application is clear for parenting and ministry as well. There are times in my life when all I believe are other people's criticisms. Then, there are those other times when I remember the positive words, and those times are an entirely different story.

More Powerful Than a Nuke

This past summer, I was talking with my friend Emadene from my hometown when I discovered that she knew my ninth-grade English teacher, Dan Johnson. Emadene had taught school with Mr. Johnson's wife and had nothing but good to say about him. When I think about his class, I have many encouraging memories. That year was truly an illustration of God moving in ways we don't understand. Mr. Johnson was a providential piece of the total equation for the man I am today.

I actually didn't start my freshman year in his class. The preceding spring, my eighth-grade English teacher had recommended that I take advanced English, so I signed up for the ninth-grade upper-level course. I was excited to be in a class with all the smart kids instead of my assumed ADHD remedial atmosphere, but at my current level, I couldn't keep up with the academic dryness of those students or a teacher who seemed to have little patience for kids like me. So I was moved out into a regular classroom. I was bummed.

But it was there, in Mr. Johnson's classroom, that I excelled. There was something different about this guy, and I finally learned in my conversation with Emadene that much of it had to do with his faith. For him, teaching English to a bunch of someone else's kids was more than a job; it was his calling. He taught pieces of life. He was created for a purpose larger than merely relaying grammatical logistics to students, and he lived that way. It's funny, but I can still conjugate the verb *to be* in all six tenses, thanks to Mr. Johnson. Who in the world knows how to conjugate the verb *to be*, much less 30 years later? I bet none of the kids in the snooty advanced English class can still do that. But I also discovered that I could write, that my imagination was a good thing, that my creativity was a noble thing.

During the last quarter of the year, we had weekly or bi-weekly creative writing assignments, and at best, I kept getting an A- on them. Finally, I asked Mr. Johnson, "What do I have to do to get an A from you?" He told me that I needed more figurative language. He told me what I needed to do, and I did it. For my last writing project, I wrote about being the hero and saving the day in a Vietnam War saga. I got an A+ on the paper. We had to read our papers out loud, and the class liked it so much that one guy made me a figure in his own adventure story. Maybe I should have asked for royalties or something.

At the end of the year, Mr. Johnson asked me if he could sign my freshman yearbook. Later, when I read his inscription, I saw the words, "To the future doctor, lawyer, professor, or statesman." Wow! How do you put a price on something like that? Here was a respected man who truly believed that I had potential, and he told me so.

I always wanted to go back to Mr. Johnson after I graduated from Bible college and let him know he had forgotten to mention preacher in his list of potential options. I never did. Emadene told me that Mr. Johnson died a number of years ago, and it struck me how important our words can be for generations to come.

I remembered the importance of acting while it's still today, for you don't know how long people have. We don't even know how long we have. I missed out on connecting with Mr. Johnson because I figured I'd eventually get around to it. But I was too late. It's not too late to think more about what I'm doing and saying today.

I don't know that we really comprehend the power of our words and encouragement. Negative words can pull a person into a pit of despair. The right words can lift a person up to be a conqueror for good.

There was a little boy who lived in our neighborhood, although he's not so little anymore. He didn't have much positive God talk in his life, so I tried to encourage him when I could. One day, we were in the front yard talking about whatever second graders talk about when the conversation turned to heroes. At that point, I told him about David and Goliath from the Bible. "And you know," I said, "one day you'll be a brave man of God just like King David was." I don't know how much the young boy took in that day, but I hope that in the future it will come back to him and he'll remember my words and be encouraged.

It's in the Being

The real power of words is more than just commenting on actions—positive or negative. It's communicating to our being. My friend Robert Tippet (RT) keeps whacking me and other people with this truth, and I think he's right. If our work defines who we are, then who we are tends to fluctuate based on how we're doing with success. The surrounding circumstances or situation can begin to define us. For a number of years, I've identified as a preacher, and I quite honestly feel like I'm a good one. I know the skill of homiletics quite well and feel passionate about what I do. But the season of depression that I went through was partly because I believed the lie that I wasn't good because I wasn't serving at a large church or a successful church plant. However, while preaching is certainly a skill and a piece of the profession, the real person—just Steve—is the same no matter where I am or what others say. The part of me that is passionate about God, his grace, and life is what raises the preacher up. Death eventually comes when the professional drive eclipses the peace of just living in the daily presence of God. RT is right, you know.

Words are important, more than we know. I find it terribly interesting that in John 1:1, the apostle John refers to Jesus Christ, the Son of God, and God in the flesh as the word. He opened his gospel like this: *"In the beginning was the Word, and the Word was with God and the Word was God"* (John 1:1).

CHAPTER 12
ECHOES OF ANOTHER REALM

Earth's crammed with heaven
and every common bush afire with God;
But only he who sees, takes off his shoes.
The rest sit round it and pluck blackberries.

—Elizabeth Barrett Browning

Either your sister is telling lies, or she is mad, or she is telling
the truth. You know she doesn't tell lies and it is obvious that
she is not mad. For the moment then and unless any further
evidence turns up, we must assume that she is telling the truth.

—C.S. Lewis (Professor Kirk
in *The Lion, the Witch, and the Wardrobe*)

We must be ready to allow ourselves to be interrupted by God.

—Dietrich Bonhoeffer

This may come as a surprise, but sometimes, I actually enjoy officiating at funerals more than weddings. I have friends in ministry who love officiating at weddings. I know an older minister who built up a good retirement after doing 30 years of weddings. My wife says I need to charge for weddings. I suppose I could, as it's pretty much a standard thing. No one would fault me if you calculate all that goes into the gig. It's quite a bit of work and quite emotionally draining. It's especially difficult for me because I care so much about what's going on and really do look at it as a sacrament, as my Catholic friends call it.

When I'm praying for the couple and asking them to make promises before God, I mean it. We really are standing here in the presence of God and asking his involvement in the proceedings and guidance and blessings of the couple. It's a real spiritual deal to me, and maybe that's why I don't charge. If people give me money, I take it. I mean, I still have two teenagers in braces. But it's like I told my wife, I wouldn't charge for baptizing someone, so why would I charge for this? Deb got that.

But I really don't like doing weddings much these days. Part of the dislike is that many aren't really taking it seriously. They're too excited and high on emotions. Don't get me wrong. I'm not a downer for weddings as a whole, and I have plenty of stories from years in the ministry. Shortly before the last wedding I officiated, the flower girl came up to me with a message from the bride and addressed me as "Hey, Mr. Head of the Show Man." I chuckled at that one. I've been called many things in my life, but that was certainly a first.

At a funeral, though, it's all ears. Why? Because it's one of those unscheduled times in our lives when all of a sudden something of eternity steps down into our pragmatic lives, reminding us that something bigger is going on here. It's not that I relish doing funerals. It's just that I know people are really paying attention and not waiting for the party or who the singles are thinking about connecting with when my boring part is over.

We also think much more deeply during funerals or when death is near. I have never been with a person near death and heard them regret not making more money or acquiring more power. If they could have changed anything, it was always a broken or unhealthy relationship.

It's sad that we have to wait until funerals or tragic events to remember that there's more to life than bank accounts and scorecards. Deep down, we know it's true, even if there isn't a funeral. We've just done a really good job of burying that truth. But when we know that we are eternal beings and that God does move among us, we think and live differently. We think about eternity and life today as a much broader picture.

Religious historians tell us that some of the Irish monks of the Middle Ages referred to the Holy Spirit as a wild goose. For the Celtic monks, the life of wild geese made a good picture of the Holy Spirit because those beautiful big birds have a mind of their own. They aren't tamable but rather unpredictable; they do what they want. In John 3, Jesus refers to the Holy Spirit as wind because you don't know where it's going.

If we're looking for the Holy Spirit, we can't think along the lines of systems and procedures. We have to be still and listen. There's a connection here to John 10:10, where Jesus states that he came that we might have life to the fullest. That principle is central to authentic Christianity. The power of following Jesus is not simply that our sins can be forgiven and that we can be with him when we die, but that we can be with him now.

The Genesis account clearly tells us that Adam and Eve regularly walked with God before they sinned. After their fall, Adam and Eve actually hid from God. They were separated from God. Many times that describes us as well. In the historical narrative, while our ancient ancestors were hiding from the divine, God was actually going to them. He still wanted a full relationship with them, and he does with us today. We tend to relegate the whole God thing to Sunday mornings or special religious events. But God wants more than that for us. That's why Jesus came, to make it possible for us to have that kind of relationship with him in the here and now. It is possible. It's possible when we pray and read his word, and it's possible when we still our minds and just listen. Like the wild geese, God doesn't allow us to dichotomize him into any system or schedule. He moves on his own time frame and in his own purposes. Our job is to listen and follow, which at times is hard to do because we typically like to lead ourselves.

It's amazing all the little ways God whispers to our souls and guides us when we're still enough and quiet enough to listen. In those times, Bible passages enter our minds from nowhere, as though God is saying, "Um, that problem that you keep worrying about, well, this is your answer in the verses you read last week."

Then come little thoughts unexpectedly throughout the day. I was frustrated recently because everything I was praying about and searching for seemed cloudy. That evening, when I was taking the dog with me to get the mail, I noted how much she was pulling on the leash and practically choking herself. I wanted to speak dog dialect to her and convey that if she'd just keep my pace, she'd get a good exercise without killing herself. Then, in a still small voice, the wild goose of the Holy Spirit gently thumped on my spirit and said, "Look who's talking, Steve." God has things under control, and many times my pain is caused by trying to pull God up to my expected pace (something I do a lot) or dragging behind him because I want to stand around sniffing useless things.

If the magic is real and that whole kingdom thing is true, then it certainly should change the way we look at life. I've been rocked over how much Jesus actually spoke about the kingdom of heaven and the kingdom of God in scripture. In the Gospel of Matthew, he referenced the kingdom of heaven 32 times, and Luke mentioned the kingdom of God just as many times. Some theologians say that the kingdom idea was central to the teaching of Christ.

The first time I really got stoked about this was back in 1992 when I was taking a class on expository preaching from Mark Scott, one of my professors at Ozark Christian College. I was studying Mark 1:15 where Jesus begins his ministry with these radical words: *"The time has come. . . . The kingdom of God has come near. Repent and believe the good news!"* The King James Version says it this way: *"The time is fulfilled, and the kingdom of God is at hand: repent ye, and believe the gospel."*

My real excitement came when I studied the original language of the verse and noticed that the phrases "time is fulfilled" and "is at hand" are both in the perfect tense. Jesus was saying that the long awaited coming of the kingdom of God was an event that happened and is continuing to happen. In other words, the kingdom of God was inaugurated with Jesus Christ, and Christ's reign continues as he rules in the lives of his citizens today and as he moves in his providential sovereignty around the world. In Luke 17:21, Jesus noted that the kingdom of God is within believers. Thus, the kingdom is anyplace his people are living in him and for him.

The kingdom is a foundational aspect of the Christian faith, but it's missing in much of America and the Western church today. Authentic Christianity is a present, daily walk with Christ that radically affects our entire lives. It changes our worldviews, our interactions with others, and our careers, marriages, churches, and life in general.

Living with an Eternal Kingdom Mindset

The truth about the kingdom also functions as an eternal filter for the decisions we make. Because I know that the fulfilled kingdom is yet to come, I can prioritize with an eternal perspective. Paul noted that because of this, we must *"fix our eyes not on what is seen, but on what is unseen, since what is seen is temporary, but what is unseen is eternal"* (2 Cor. 4:18). With that in mind, we're forced to rethink what life and success look like in the grand scheme of things.

Kingdom Success

My friend Doug said I was not entrepreneurial enough to accomplish the vision I put before him. While I believe his overall assessment was off, I'm okay with it now because I truly believe that God is always working in ways we can't see. I still sometimes feel funny whenever I see or hear the word *entrepreneurship*. It's a confusing word not only because it's hard to spell but also because of the many word pictures that come with it.

Businesses and marketplaces are usually the venues for entrepreneurship. The word can be applied equally to someone who starts up a business and someone who takes an existing company to the next level. I swim mostly in the realm of church and discipleship where the range of applications can be just as wide. A church planter establishes one church in his life that grows to 1,000 or more in Sunday morning attendance, so he's allowed to wear the title. Someone else takes an existing ministry to new heights and is awarded the spotlight for his accomplishments. The bigger the results, the more a person earns the title *entrepreneur*. Those who achieve lesser accolades are denied the label.

I wonder if maybe there's more to the story here in creativity. Could it be that for divine entrepreneurship to happen, we need a number of different people, different skills, and different situations?

To illustrate, I'm wondering who's the biggest entrepreneur in the fast food business, the McDonald brothers or Ray Kroc? The original McDonald's drive-in restaurant opened in 1937 in Pasadena, California. The brothers struck gold. They expanded and were hitting revenue of $350,000 per year in the mid-1950s. Kroc came into the picture in 1954 with a business that sold milkshake machines. He had a vision for what McDonalds could be, and in 1961, he bought the franchise rights for $2.7 million.

The rest is history. Franchises opened all over the world, including the ones I ate at in Moscow, Russia. When you look at these men, who is the greater entrepreneur? Many would say Kroc since he was the greater visionary. Others say it was the McDonald brothers who were better managers. In one sense, I agree with team Kroc. On the other hand, Kroc would have gotten nowhere without the original entrepreneurship of Dick and Maurice McDonald. Both were needed, but we don't always see that when our eyes are constantly focused on the celebrity of entrepreneurship.

That is also the case in the kingdom of God. There are so many pieces that come into play with the expansion of the kingdom. We all have different gifts, some more bent on creating and others focused on organizing programs. Even in those, there is an element of vision to carry projects to the next level. We also have to consider circumstances, timing, and a number of other factors. When it comes to church planting, I think of the apostle Paul who experienced various levels of success as recorded in the book of Acts. If we knew only of his ministry in Athens in Acts 17, we might not consider him a worthy entrepreneur. The text tells us that only a few became followers of Christ (Acts 17:34 TLB). But in chapter 19, the entire city of Ephesus turned upside down at Paul's preaching of Christ. Paul was the same man in both places. Quite possibly, the experts of the day could have said that Paul failed in one and was successful in the other, but we know the truth—Paul was successful in God's sight by simply pressing forward and leaving the results to God.

Maybe that can be an encouragement to you in your sphere of influence. We all possess some aspect of entrepreneurship because we are all daughters and sons of Adam and Eve. God charged his first children with not only naming the animals but governing creation.

We are all created in God's image, and God is creative. So while the experts in your field may never call you to speak at their national convention, keep in mind that there is more at play than we realize. God's plan has all of us in mind, and there is a creative side to each one of his children. The real test of entrepreneurial success is simply what we do with what God has placed in our hands.

This topic reminds me of a guy named Morris. I like to call him Saint Morris these days. I met Morris for the first time on an inner-city college trip in Atlanta in the spring of 1989. Then I went to college with him when I transferred to Ozark Christian College that fall. But Morris went home to be with Christ a few years ago after faithfully serving God for a number of years in Honduras. When I got the note from some dear friends in Tegucigalpa, Honduras, I paused for a long time. I sensed God's faithfulness, and I knew in that moment that Morris was now enjoying his eternal reward. Here's what struck me: Morris was never a flashy guy by the world's standards, and he suffered from various sicknesses throughout his life. Because of that, Morris was unfortunately never going to be invited to talk at a big convention. Sadly, most people didn't see a lot in him.

Yet here's the real deal on Morris. He was a guy giving all he had to follow Christ and speak up for him in whatever way he could. He was dedicated. He lived and breathed kingdom principles. He will never get people's applause or accolades here on earth. But now he's experiencing his great reward. When I got the news of Morris going home, I felt that he was what Jesus was talking about when he said that *"the last will be first, and the first will be last"* (Matt. 20:16).

Many people say they want to be like someone great. They want to emulate a president, a great athlete, or a superstar preacher. But I wonder how different things would be if we all followed the lead of a guy named Morris.

Heaven on My Mind

It's not only when I'm leading a funeral service that I think about heaven. There are divine moments throughout life when heaven comes to mind, such as when I'm reading C. S. Lewis or J. R. R. Tolkien, or watching one of their great masterpieces on film. *The Lion, the Witch, and the Wardrobe* and *The Lord of the Rings* totally set the stage for another realm beyond what we can touch today.

Heaven comes to mind when I'm scanning the dial on a road trip and something like U2's "Where the Streets Have No Name" comes on. I'm again reminded that I'm part of something so much bigger than the here and now.

Sometimes, heaven comes out of my plea for God to make things right. I see the evil and rebellion in the world, and my heart cries out for justice. Then, I know that justice will come someday.

Sometimes, it comes as a calm and positive reminder of what lies in store for me beyond the veil. I've often joked that my mansion in heaven will have four huge windows on the four exterior walls. One will face a new Lake Tahoe (like that would need any improvement) and the Sierra Mountains in the background, followed by the much higher Rocky Mountains with their peaks crowned with snow only when I wanted it that way. The second window will reveal what I remember from my time in Australia, a landscape with all the foliage and birds and animal life. The third will open over the Pacific Coast, but the water will be just as warm as the Gulf of Mexico. And the fourth will look out to an ever-expanding rolling prairie like what I remember growing up in the Texas Panhandle.

Imagine a time long ago when the buffalo roamed the Plains from Texas all the way up to Canada. I've not actually seen it, but I can almost feel the ground shaking as massive herds of these huge creatures crossed the grasslands. There is something about those vast tracks of open land that seem to whisper, "I'm big, dangerous, and beyond your control, so don't even try to mess with me." It's kind of like looking up into the cosmos, which is really easy in the Plains, and seeing that there is no end to space. It's almost haunting with its never-ending expanse. I joke about my home in heaven, but there is some truth to that. I could live in a house like that in heaven and experience the power and beauty of God's creation every day.

Heaven is anything but boring. The old idea of sitting around singing is a far cry from heavenly reality. Whatever the specifics are of this heaven Jesus spoke of and the mansion he's preparing, they will be quite the adventure of never-ending horizons.

Our ultimate goal is not here. The final score is not settled in this life. Because of that, we can readjust our thinking to a much bigger picture. The apostle Paul encouraged the first Christians to *"set your hearts on things above, where Christ is, seated at the right hand of God. Set your minds on things above, not on earthly things. For you died, and your life is now hidden with Christ in God. When Christ, who is your life, appears, then you also will appear with him in glory"* (Col. 3:1–4).

When I officiate at funerals, the joyous times come when we're celebrating the life of a saint who has walked with the Lord for many, many years. With family members at the funeral home or at the graveside, I often read one of my favorite passages on this subject—Revelation 21:1–4. The context is a revelation given to the apostle John in the final days of his life on earth. John was in exile on the island of Patmos, which may have been a Roman penal colony. He had been physically persecuted and was now separated by the sea from his friends and family. He was utterly alone. But then the glorified Christ visited him and gave him a vision of things to come.

I'm not a big scholar or mighty theologian on the book of Revelation. There are many things I still don't get in this profoundly deep book. But what I do know is that one of the central themes is coming home. At the end of it all, we get to go home. That is what John experienced, and I'll just let him speak for himself:

Then I saw "a new heaven and a new earth," for the first heaven and the first earth had passed away, and there was no longer any sea. I saw the Holy City, the new Jerusalem, coming down out of heaven from God, prepared as a bride beautifully dressed for her husband. And I heard a loud voice from the throne saying, "Look! God's dwelling place is now among the people, and he will dwell with them. They will be his people, and God himself will be with them and be their God. 'He will wipe every tear from their eyes. There will be no more death' or mourning or crying or pain, for the old order of things has passed away" (Rev. 21:1–4).

Did you catch that last phrase? "For the old order of things has passed away." I can almost hear and see it when I take time to be still and listen. And then, almost like an echo, I can hear the words of Jesus: *"Well done, good and faithful servant! You have been faithful with a few things; I will put you in charge of many things. Come and share your master's happiness!"* (Matt. 25:23).

CONCLUSION
THE METAMORPHOSIS REALLY DOES HAPPEN

Let your religion be less of a theory
and more of a love affair.

—G.K. Chesterton

We . . . are being transformed into his image
with ever-increasing glory.

—Apostle Paul to the Corinthians

The door on which we have been knocking
all our lives will open at last.

—C.S. Lewis

Yes, it's true. I'm not the same man who left California in the
summer of 2009 with my heart lost in a dark canyon. I'm also not
the guy who left my hometown for Bible college in 1989. In fact,
I'm really not the guy I was yesterday. But I am, indeed, still the
guy who God created and envisioned in the first place—just Steve,
not Pastor Steve. My passion for Jesus and hunger for life have not
changed; they have grown. That real, true part of me will never
change. God made me that way.

When I say I'm not the same guy, I'm referring to all the stupid decisions I made and all the ways I stumbled and fell. Indeed, I'm healthier today because Jesus has changed me over time. We'll never be perfect, and I pity the person who shoots for that goal. But as we experience a new birth in Jesus and purposefully pursue him, he changes us. It's a process that sometimes takes a while, but it does happen.

The Daily Decisions and Eternal Transformations

I'm not a country-western fan. In fact, I like to tell people that God created music, and then Satan made an attempt at it that resulted in country-western. I enjoy so many different genres, from classical to Christian hard rock (head-banger music is what our church administrative assistant calls it). I've picked up a love for Irish, Scottish, and English folk music lately, and sometimes old traditional Russian music finds its way to my Pandora stations. I thread a little classic rock through my week as well. But I just can't make the switch to country-western. Okay, maybe some John Denver once in a while, but that's probably a bit more folk than western. Country music and I just don't do business with each other.

My wife, however, grew up on the country twang. Many of those songs bring her fond memories and set her at ease. I don't naturally like country, but she does. So what do we listen to on the car radio? It's mostly a compromise of Christian rock, worship songs, or some kind of talk show. There are times when I put on specifically what I want, and then there are times, like last Sunday night, when I make a conscious decision to find exactly what she wants. Then, young country flows through our 2005 Honda Odyssey sound system for the rest of the evening.

I don't get it right all the time, and many times I get it totally wrong. But there are times that I do get it right, and the cool thing is that those are becoming more frequent. Jesus said that he came to serve, not to be served. In those moments in the car, that's exactly what I strive for: to make a deliberate choice to serve my wife.

It's those day-by-day and moment-by-moment decisions that determine life. While there are definitely defining moments that may change the course of our lives or even history, it's the daily decisions that really produce character—who we are and who we are becoming.

In Christian theology, there are two terms that come to mind. The first is *salvation,* and the second is *sanctification.* Salvation occurs when we step across the line to follow Jesus and change our citizenship from this world to the kingdom of heaven. Jesus referred to it as being born again (John 3).

Sanctification is the ongoing process in which followers of Jesus are slowly transformed into his image. The word *sanctification* refers to something or someone who is set aside or apart for a particular purpose. The Old Testament priests would sanctify precious items for the temple.

When it comes to people, the scriptures are clear that this process is something God works in us. We see it in 2 Thessalonians 2:13 and 1 Peter 1:2, where the apostles speak of the sanctifying work of the Holy Spirit. In 1 Corinthians 6:11, the apostle Paul noted powerfully that those in Jesus are washed, sanctified, and justified. There is a real sense of Christ-followers being set aside for a grand purpose.

There are also texts such as 1 Thessalonians 4:3 where we're reminded that it is God's will that we should be sanctified by the choices we make. As we make those choices for Jesus, Paul assures us that we are daily being transformed into the image of Jesus with ever-increasing glory. The more we humbly walk with him on a daily basis, the more we become like him.

Salvation is not something you earn. Ephesians 2:8–10 clearly shows that our salvation is the gracious result of what Jesus did on the cross for us. My hope of salvation does not rest in my performance, but in Christ. He paid my debt.

Sanctification is a gradual transformation into becoming more like Jesus. It's kind of like eventually becoming like the people you hang around with the most. By living out my salvation, I'm being sanctified by a regular abiding in his presence. Sure, I'm not there yet. But the daily decision to say yes to Jesus is what makes us become more like Jesus.

And who knows? The more we make sacrificial decisions to listen to our spouse's country music, the more we might actually find some songs we like—well, maybe.

I Am the Lord's Servant

We read about it at least once a year, sometime around Christmas, when we think about Mary and Joseph and baby Jesus. One tradition I picked up from my mother is reading the birth narratives of Jesus on Christmas morning before we open presents. I've preached on it countless times in one way or another.

But let's look at the angel Gabriel who showed up in a little Hebrew town to deliver God's message—that God had found favor with Mary to make her the mother of the promised Messiah, the hope of humanity. A lot of preachers talk about it around Christmas, but I'm not really sure we understand all that Mary was laying on the line. Sure, she was compromising her reputation and possibly her life since the religious legalists could have stoned her for being pregnant before marriage. But she was also risking her own hopes and dreams. We can only assume what was going through her mind and emotions when the divine announcement came. Had she been dreaming about a big and festive wedding since she was a little girl?

What we do know is that after the announcement, she responded with a quiet and trusting response to God: *"I am the Lord's servant. . . . May your word to me be fulfilled"* (Luke 1:38). Although we don't see it in the text, I can imagine the peace on Mary's face. I don't think she responded through clenched teeth as I do at times.

Mary had a humble and trusting heart. She exhibited real, authentic faith in her complete trust in God. It's trust and submission to Jesus, even when life doesn't make sense, that transforms us.

It's not always a picture-perfect path. Sometimes, we get lost; we take wrong turns. Looking at the biblical history and text, even Mary didn't always get it right. Later, when Jesus began his earthly ministry, Mary and the rest of Jesus's earthly family thought he was nuts (Mark 3:21). They couldn't comprehend what God was doing and fell back on their own reasoning.

I've been there. When life just doesn't make sense and I can't understand what God's doing, I lean on my own understanding and work my own agenda. I override his plan by trying to take control.

There are others who didn't always take the right turns, yet we still lift them up as examples of faith. Abraham lied about his wife to save himself and saw his son, Isaac, do the same thing years later. Peter denied Jesus. Paul had to repent after being too hard on young Mark. Throughout the Bible, the greatest women and men of faith fell down from time to time.

Here's a fun fact about the hall of famers in Hebrews 11. Samson is included among them. Samson? What do we know about this guy? If we took Arnold Schwarzenegger, Chuck Norris, and Sylvester Stallone and rolled them into one guy, we might get a glimpse of who Samson was. The boy was big. In the history of Samson, it's clear that he had a great future ahead of him (Judges 13:1–5). God chose him to lead his people and uniquely gifted him for the task. He had a bright future, and he blew it.

He saw a lady he had the hots for, but she wasn't a follower of God. Intellectually, he may have known this was an issue, but he wanted her anyway and figured he could handle the tension. Despite the pleas of his family, Samson took confidence in his own strength and judgment and insisted on getting his own way. In doing so, his falling led to his failing. If you've not read the whole story, it's really one of simple rebellion against God, inflated self-confidence, and arrogance. He wound up in prison as a slave to the enemies of God. He had a future, but he fell and failed miserably.

But that's not where his life ended. In Judges 16, Samson experienced total brokenness and humbled himself before God. His tormentors had plucked out his eyes and held him captive, but he used his last ounce of strength and breath to praise God and bring about a final victory. He killed more of Israel's enemies in his death than in his life. Maybe in those final moments of his life he realized that his real strength came from faith and not from flesh. We know he practiced faith, for he's listed among the great men of faith in Hebrews 11:32, which is no small deal. His faith overcame his failure.

I'm encouraged by this, and I hope you are as well when you feel intimidated by your imperfection. We have to move forward, day by day, even when we don't get it right. Pressing on is the biggest part of faith. Many times, when we talk about stepping out in faith, we think of missionaries or a Green Beret kind of Christian who takes radical risks for the kingdom. Yes, there is a huge amount of faith involved in leaving a job for the mission field or giving up a lucrative career to become a servant at a local church. But sometimes, the biggest act of faith is putting one foot in front of the other when no one knows what's going on and you just can't seem to see the fruit. Even the saints in scripture experienced days, months, and years of waiting. We love and are inspired by accounts such as David and Goliath, Peter's miraculous escape from jail, or Paul's vision of the man from Macedonia. But we forget all those years David ran from King Saul in the wilderness, Peter stumbled in faith, and Paul waited in Tarsus or a Roman jail.

For a while, I wondered about my faith when I saw other preachers doing life with perpetual smiles on their faces. I had a smile, but it was fake. Maybe their smiles were fake, too, or maybe those other guys just had more faith than I did. Maybe I wasn't as strong and faithful as those guys, especially the ones at bigger churches or more successful ministries. I also wondered if they would be that happy if all their dreams and plans fell through.

Much of my problem was that I was listening to Satan's lies. Real faith doesn't have anything to do with big results in the eyes of the world; it's trusting God no matter what. And part of trusting God is intentionally seeing what he's doing and what he's done.

After Mary received Gabriel's message from God, she sang praises to him. Despite the trouble she would soon experience, she trusted and actively worshiped him. There are times when we have to intentionally choose to thank God for what we do know and trust him for the rest.

Just Do It

Sometimes, the best thing to do when you're at the end of the rope is to trust God and just do the next thing. A while back on a Sunday afternoon, I was physically exhausted and emotionally spent after preaching that morning. I was also handling a number of church projects and concerns that felt like a mountaineering backpack filled with lead, all the while knowing I had an important meeting that night. But after a short crash on my bed and watching my favorite football team get beat, I threw some water on my face, stood still for a moment, asked Jesus for physical help, and put one foot in front of the other.

We don't see that a lot in the Bible, but that's pretty much what life is. We like the action stories of David whopping Goliath, but we silently ignore all the days that David was in the desert waiting on God. Eventually, God worked through that normal Hebrew teenager who was stepping out in faith on a daily basis.

It was a good meeting and teaching time that Sunday night. I was still physically beat when I got home, but there was more of a smile on my face than when I left. I'm not sure what caused the positive change in my demeanor that night. It could have been something as simple as the additional dopamine in my brain chemistry caused by the physical action of getting up and moving. Maybe it was a swath of encouragement from the Holy Spirit. Or maybe it was just a sense that if I kept climbing, I'd eventually reach the summit of the mountain, and that's a good thought.

The World before Us

I don't have it all figured out. I don't know where I'll be a year from now or even when I'm 70. But this I know: Jesus loves me. Ministry is worth it, God is moving, and lives are being changed—and that's something to press on for.

In his second letter to the church in Corinth, the apostle Paul speaks of being transformed into the image of Christ with ever-increasing glory (2 Cor. 3:18). The more we abide in Jesus and follow him, the more we become like him. It's a process, and I can see that happening in my heart.

I'm even okay being a nice pastor these days. I'm good with that, and I don't internalize it as a negative anymore—most of the time. I got a rude e-mail a couple of weeks ago. Someone was blaming me for something I hadn't done over an issue that wasn't a serious problem. When I received the electronic tirade, I didn't go either way with it. I didn't blow up at the person, and I didn't let it depress me. It was what it was, and it was not my fault. There was no need to bonk the person on the head, and who really cared if he was right or wrong? In the past, it would have deflated me. The little kid in me may have spoken up, reminded of all the times I had been falsely accused and that this was just more of the same. Maybe it was more of the same, but I wasn't the same.

There were a couple of options available to me in that moment. I could believe the person's attack, which I had a track record of doing, or I could crucify the person, letting him know that he was wrong. In the end, I did neither.

It's a lot easier to move forward in life when you're at peace with God, yourself, and others. When you're still, completely at home in his presence, no matter what's going on around you, you're free to move mountains.

Leaving a Legacy

It was early September 2017, and I was at my home office computer watching the live-streamed memorial service of one of the men who had encouraged me in ministry. His name was Roy Wheeler, and he served in Amarillo, Texas, for more than 40 years as the senior minister of Hillside Christian Church (Paramount Terrace Christian Church when I was growing up). My first two suits came from Roy. They were a necessity back then for being a preacher. In April 1994, in my senior year of college, Roy came up to Joplin, Missouri, to hear me preach what was called a senior sermon, delivered to the student body, faculty, and staff, and then participate in my ordination service for full-time Christian ministry. Later that day, Roy said he was so impressed with my sermon that he wanted me to come back to Paramount Terrace Christian Church and preach it for all three Sunday morning services before Debi and I left for Moscow, Russia.

I wanted to be at his memorial service, but with all the hurricane relief our Houston area church was engaged in, I couldn't make it happen. I'm sure that among all the people in attendance, there were men like me who owed part of their journey in Christian ministry to Roy. While it was Jesus who truly called me to this task, it was Roy and men like him who confirmed it. For that, I am ever grateful.

The afternoon of his memorial service was one of those times in the race of our lives when we stop and think about all those who have been a positive influence on us. For me, the A team of mentors in my life are Roy, Eric Wolfram, Max Goins, Mark Scott, Fred Masteller, Dennis Platt, Bob Gerhardt, and Steve Sigler. Take time to remember, thank Jesus for, and possibly reach out to those who have encouraged you.

Because we live in such a negative culture, the positive power of the tongue is such a rarity. I often ask myself whom I might encourage as these men have encouraged me. What about you? Someday, you and I will be center stage at a funeral or memorial service. At that time, who will stop and thank Jesus for your life?

The Joy Is Greater

The other day, I got an e-mail from a guy named Jeff in the Sacramento area. I met Jeff a number of years ago when I was canvassing a new neighborhood for our church plant. God had been working in his heart for a while, and I happened to come by at the right time. Jeff decided to follow Jesus, but life took us down different paths. He moved to another part of Sacramento, Debi and I moved back to the Midwest, and I have not seen Jeff since. But his e-mail showed up in my inbox, and I was encouraged to see everything God was doing in his life. Jeff is now walking with Jesus and part of a great church family.

Every now and then, I get a call from Aaron Price. Aaron is an officer with the Indiana Highway Patrol, but I remember him as a young man I spent time with when Debi and I served in that part of the country. I had the privilege of performing his wedding before we moved from Indiana to California in 2004. It always brings a smile to my face to think of these people and all that God is doing in their lives. There are others as well. The list goes on and on.

I've encouraged younger men who are now in the ministry, some in much larger churches than mine and others in different parts of the world. Some couples have lived out great marriages and served in churches because of the influence God has allowed Debi and me to have on their lives. I see today the beautiful growth and outlook of our church family on the northwest side of Houston that did not exist when we came here a few years ago.

When I think about a legacy, I think of those people who were teenagers when I first met them and now have families of their own. What kind of faith is being transmitted to those young hearts even now, and who will come behind them?

Remembering stories and people from Russia, Indiana, California, Houston, and everywhere else I've been brings joy to my heart. It's reminds me again and again that God is still moving in ways we can't see and that he is, indeed, faithful.

A legacy is also a testimony that God pays attention and that there is value in all we do. In 1 Corinthians 15:58, Paul exhorts the first church to *"always give yourselves fully to the work of the Lord, because you know that your labor in the Lord is not in vain."*

I'm thinking of Samson again. I wonder how his life could have been different. I also wonder how ours can be different today. The truth is that no matter where we've been or what we've done, Jesus still has plans for us. The more we press into him and rely on our brothers and sisters in Christ, the more God can use us. We don't need to have the body mass of Samson or the gifts of others. We just need to know that real strength comes through faith and not flesh. No matter who we are, what we have or haven't done, God has a plan for us to co-create with him a better world now and in the fulfilled kingdom in heaven.

The joy of following Jesus is greater and the promises of Jesus are more profound than we can possibly realize. I may or may not see all my dreams fulfilled in this life, and that's okay. God sees the bigger picture. He sees things I cannot see, and he knows those who will come after me. When it's all said and done, God is faithful. When we reach the finish line, it's more than worth it. So press on in the fight, my friend. It will be worth it for you, too.

ACKNOWLEDGMENTS

If you are holding a copy of *Confessions* in your hand right now, it is because of Michael Cusick and Dr. Eriko Valk. It was their encouragement and formal confirmation in my casual writing that brought this project to fruition. My deepest thanks to you both for verbalizing your belief in me.

Thank you to my official "unofficial" review team. You were the first to graciously review early sections of the material and respond with encouragement to press on. Thanks to Mary Barlow, Lori Foster, Nancy Green, Ruthie Gallo, Eric Hinton, Leo Lopez, Stephen Miles, Kimberly Stetzel, Jim Tune, Judy Wolfram, and Nitermosquiter.

A fun shout-out to Angie Kiesling for her first professional thoughts. Thanks especially to Laura Allnutt for her formal and professional editing work and for challenging me toward more professionalism in writing. My compliments to Sue Vander Hook for putting the final proofreading touches on everything.

My sincere thanks to the kickstarter production team for making this project financially viable. Special thanks to key producers Jon Glaze, Leo Lopez, Andrew McLeod, Rick and Jeanne Thompson, and Patty Turner. My humble gratitude to executive producers Robert and Brenda Galvan, Chris and Lynn Jackson, Dave R, and David Hinton.

Thanks to those who logistically made this project possible. From John Hinton crafting the kickstarter video to Sammantha and everyone on the Lucid production staff. Thanks to Laurie Waller of Lucid for your guidance and grace and just being fun to work with. I am immensely grateful for my church family at Cypress Crossings Christian Church for their love and for giving me the time to create this project. I pray that together we might see more people come to know the love of Jesus Christ.

A shout-out to my sons, John and David, of whom I'm very proud. A *"Blurp"* to my girls, Esther and Abigail, who bring such joy to my life. I am so proud of you and am greatly blessed to be your father. Most importantly, a profound thank you to The Debster, who has been editing my work since college when she said "I do" in front of God and witnesses. You are not only my chief editor but also my closest friend and will ever and always be the "wife of my youth." I cannot thank you enough.

NOTES

Foreword

1. David Hansen, *The Art of Pastoring: Ministry Without All the Answers* (Downers Grove, IL: Intervarsity Press, 2012), 66.
2. Jonna-Lynn K. Mandelbaum, *Unspoken Farewell* (Indianapolis, IN: Dog Ear Publishing, 2008), 130.

Chapter 1

1. Audio Adrenaline, "Man of God," *Bloom* (Memphis, TN: Ardent Recordings, 1996).
2. *The Boy in the Plastic Bubble*, Directed by Randal Kleiser, ABC Television Network. 1976.

Chapter 2

1. Bruce Marshall, *The World, The Flesh, and Father Smith* (Scotland: Houghton Mifflin Co, 1945), 108.

Chapter 3

1. Rich Mullins, "Boy Like Me/Man Like You," *The World as Best as I Remember It*, Reunion Records, 1991.

Chapter 4

1. Kay S. Hymowitz, "Where Have the Good Men Gone?" *Wall Street Journal*, February 19, 2011, https://www.wsj.com/articles/SB10001424 052748704409004576146321725889448.

2. Jennifer Fink, "Why Schools Are Failing Our Boys," *Washington Post*, February 19, 2015, https://www.washingtonpost.com/news/parenting/wp/2015/02/19/why-schools-are-failing-our-boys/?noredirect=on&utm_term=.a8e2bc9613ce.

Chapter 7

1. Abraham Lincoln, "Letter to John Stuart (January 23, 1841)," *Lincoln's Writings: The Multi-Media Edition*, http://housedivided.dickinson.edu/sites/lincoln/letter-to-john-stuart-january-23-1841/.

Chapter 8

1. Hudson Taylor, quoted in Mike Pettingill, "God's Work, God's Way," *The Gospel Coalition*, https://www.thegospelcoalition.org/article/gods-work-gods-way/.

Chapter 10

1. *Glory Road*, directed by James Gartner, The Walt Disney Company, 2006.

Chapter 11

1. Derived from Neil T. Anderson, *The Bondage Breaker* (Eugene, OR: Harvest House Publishers, 2000).
2. *The Help*, directed by Tate Taylor, DreamWorks, 2011.

ABOUT THE AUTHOR

Steve Hinton has been in full-time Christian ministry for nearly 25 years. He has served as a missionary in Russia, a church planter in California, and a preaching minister for two local Christian churches in Indiana and Houston. Steve is a graduate of Ozark Christian College with Bachelor of Biblical Literature and Bachelor of Theology degrees. He received his Master of Practical Ministries from Cincinnati Christian Seminary. He continues to engage in world evangelism.

Steve is also just a regular guy who has struggled with issues of faith like the rest of us. In his book, he has shed the religious mask and connected real life and real faith. He has been married to Debi for 27 years, and they have four children. Steve enjoys God's creation and likes to tell people that one of the windows in his mansion in heaven will look out onto a new Lake Tahoe. Steve regularly blogs and includes weekly videos on his kingdomology.org website.

CPSIA information can be obtained
at www.ICGtesting.com
Printed in the USA
FSHW01n1504141018
52939FS